The Press and

Restaurant Guide

The Essential Guide to Eating Out
in Aberdeen and around Scotland

Edited by Sonja Cox

BLACK & WHITE PUBLISHING

First published 2009
by Black & White Publishing Ltd
29 Ocean Drive, Edinburgh EH6 6JL

ISBN: 978 1 84502 252 5

Previously published in the *Press & Journal* 2006–2009

A CIP catalogue record for this book is available from the British Library.

DISCLAIMER
The information in this guide was gathered between 2006 and 2009 and previously published in
the *Press and Journal*. The content is provided in good faith but no guarantee or representation is
given by the publisher that the material is accurate, complete or up-to-date.

Typeset by Ellipsis Books Limited, Glasgow
Printed and bound by MPG Books Ltd, Bodmin

Contents

Introduction

Welcome to our pick of the best restaurants recently reviewed by the *Press and Journal*'s undercover team of food writers.

The critics travel the length and breadth of the north and north-east of Scotland in search of culinary perfection.

Although appearances and reputations can be deceptive when judging restaurants, star quality shines through. The quality of the food, creation of innovative dishes and sourcing of local produce were critical, of course, but the standard of menu, service, value for money, surroundings and location took equal share of the marks in the final assessment by the writers.

Having a passion for food and attention to every detail, both at the front of house and in the kitchen, seems to be the recipe for success for all of the best establishments.

Enjoy the table of delights we have laid out before you – and bon appétit.

Bistro Verde
The Green, Aberdeen

telephone: 01224 586180

"Top green cuisine"

It was a Thursday night in Aberdeen and we fancied a bite to eat – something different from the norm yet laid-back enough to allow us to relax and kick back.

We decided upon **Bistro Verde** on the Green, located in a historic part of the Granite City.

It doesn't have many pretensions, but quietly goes about its business with the hustle and bustle of Union Street just yards above.

Aberdeen's connection with fishing and the sea is sometimes overlooked these days as technology and the oil industry loom large.

But **Bistro Verde** prides itself on its fresh seafood, and if you're looking for somewhere to go to enjoy it, you'd be hard pushed to surpass this establishment.

Pale wood dominates the interior, with deep blue walls adding to the marine theme, and at night, it is atmospherically lit with fairy lights and candles.

It's not particularly spacious, but makes the most of what it has. And what it does have room for is a specials board crammed full of goodies.

As well as an à la carte menu which is quite mouthwatering enough, the specials encompass yet more fishy options designed to make your choice that little bit harder.

But I always think this is a good sign of the freshness of what's on offer, so along with the delights of the main menu, we got stuck into choosing.

Seafood obviously dominates, with Cajun-style red snapper, grilled halibut, smoked salmon, trout and sea bass, but they also jostle with the likes of Greek-style platters with feta and olives, and stuffed chestnut mushrooms.

All the dishes are imaginatively put together with lashings of fresh lemon or dill, or perhaps some chilli and spring onion, or fresh ratatouille.

The emphasis is on sparkling seasonal flavours which complement the main event.

I went for a favourite of mine, seared king scallops, which were served with slices of the tiniest black pudding. They were described recently to me as fishy marshmallows, but I haven't allowed this to colour my judgment.

These were moist and bouncy and the freshest of the fresh.

Across from me was grilled sea bass teetering on a tower of baby new potatoes, served with spinach with a bit of a peppery kick. All was declared delicious.

For main course, I picked the char-grilled tuna with Caprese salad

drizzled with white truffle oil, the huge blobs of mozzarella nestling underneath.

I asked for it rare and I would say it was heading for the medium side of rare, but it still melted in the mouth, the char-grilled pattern studded with crushed peppercorns.

The menu revels in seafood, but does offer other options for those who aren't entirely convinced by fish.

The specials board was hit once more by my dining companion with the chicken, which lay white and tender on a bed of fluffy herb mash and came along with the ubiquitous black pudding accompaniment.

It was beautifully presented and just as well proportioned, and my companion seemed fully satisfied by the wholesome flavours from the combination of chicken, potato and gravy.

There were certainly potatoes aplenty as, along with the aforementioned herb mash, there were dauphinoise as well as sliced new potatoes in the side dish. It was just the right amount to share with courgettes, carrots, sugar snap peas and baby corn, all cooked wonderfully al dente.

For desserts, the warm chocolate sponge came with proper vanilla-specked ice cream. The sight of the huge slab being transported across the room was slightly daunting, but we were assured it was very light.

It certainly vanished from the plate like the proverbial snow off a dyke.

Other options included sticky toffee crème brûlée, white chocolate and Baileys cheesecake, roasted figs with ice cream or a healthy-looking cheese and biscuit selection which was shared by the table next to us.

I went for what I usually regard as the soft option of the ice cream. But this came in a charmingly retro home-made brandy-snap basket and consisted of more of the smooth vanilla, some piquant pistachio and gingerbread flavour. Now I don't know who came up with the concept of gingerbread ice cream, but it is inspired. Its warm fudginess just melted into the brandy snap. A match made in heaven.

The service was some of the best I've come across in Aberdeen. From the warm welcome on the phone during our admittedly rather last-minute booking to the choice of tables on our arrival, to the assistance when ordering, right through to the advice on where we could dance the night away on leaving, I really couldn't have faulted the waitresses. They were intuitive and charming without being in any way cloying or insincere.

So although we were drawn by the relaxed, informal vibe, don't be fooled. There are some great things at work in this kitchen, blended together with excellent front-of-house service.

Quality of Food	5
Menu Choice	4
Surroundings	4
Location	5
Service	5
Value for Money	4
Total *[out of 30]*	**27**

The Broadstraik Inn
Elrick, Westhill, Aberdeen

telephone: 01224 743217   website: www.broadstraikinn.co.uk

"Just perfect"

I knew we had enjoyed a lovely night at the **Broadstraik Inn** as my mother was asking a manager if she could book the exact same table for our next visit.

This struck me as an odd thing to do by Annie Galvin (for that was the name she was born with on Ireland's fair shores 76 years ago, but I can't give her married name because that would blow my cover, of course).

It seemed strange to be asking about booking a table as she lived 450 miles away and was hardly likely to be popping back to the Broadstraik soon.

Anyway, it's the thought that counts and she was still basking in the warmth of good food, surroundings and service.

The **Broadstraik**, just a few miles out of Aberdeen, had taken us by surprise. It looked like any other country pub of a certain age on the outside, but was offering something much more than pub grub inside.

Perhaps it should not have been a surprise given the pedigree of the people behind it. **Broadstraik** is owned by Jackie Spence and husband Chris Wills. Jackie's father, Stewart Spence, is well known for his top class Marcliffe Hotel on the outskirts of Aberdeen, while Chris's father, George Wyatt, owns the popular La Lombarda Italian restaurant in Aberdeen.

The couple also used to run The Eating Room restaurant in Aberdeen and staff followed them to the new venture. That is some background, eh?

We discovered quickly that this little gem sparkles with excellent food at very reasonable prices. It turned out to be a wise thing to do to book in advance as it was busy throughout our Friday night visit. It also attracted all ages. There were small groups like ours (me, mum and wife), young families with children, senior citizens and couples in the 30-something range.

The spacious dining-room had tables laid out along the walls, often snuggling in nice little alcoves, some through the middle and more on a raised area at the far end.

Soft lights and framed paintings of local rural scenes helped create a relaxed atmosphere. There was also a decent gap between the tables, which is something I like to see. I don't want to seem standoffish, but I don't like being so close to my fellow diners that I can hear their opinions drowning out, well, my opinions.

There were plenty of waiting staff around and they were very attentive at working the tables and checking if everything was OK. How often do you sit down to eat elsewhere and think you have

suddenly become invisible to the staff?

As we were studying the menus, I was conscious of one of the waitresses slowly easing an extra chair between me and my mother. I knew they were busy, but surely they were not going to put someone else at our table?

Luckily, she was just using it as a prop for a large blackboard listing the **Broadstraik's** specials.

Our eyes were darting between the menu and the blackboard, both offering some interesting choices.

I kicked off proceedings with smoked haddock risotto; my wife chose breaded brie with salad and cranberry and orange chutney, while mother was quite taken with the yellow split pea and vegetable soup.

I was looking forward to the risotto as I did not recall ever having tried a smoked haddock version in the past. It did not disappoint and lit up the table with its vibrant golden sheen in the bowl. It did not have the fluffiness of some risottos, but was quite a sticky, creamy fusion of fish and rice. I loved its texture, I have to say, and it was bursting with flavours.

My wife's brie was a nice contrast. She opened up the crispy outer coating and the brie flowed out temptingly on to the plate. These were both dishes I would not have expected here. My mother's hearty and generous

5

serving of soup also received her seal of approval.

On to mains and, for me, lamb cutlets with sweet mash and sauteed carrots and beans. My wife opted for an 8oz sirloin steak with a large Portobello mushroom and baked potato, while mum had pesto-baked chicken with couscous, tomatoes and courgettes.

When these dishes arrived at the table, we were all struck by how well they were presented and served on attractive dishes and plates. It was worth a few seconds to just admire the effort in preparing them before tucking in. The look was certainly matched by the excellent taste combinations across each plate.

The size of the portions was also on the generous side and my mother had to give up out of sheer exhaustion in the end as she battled with a tender, succulent pesto-flavoured serving of chicken.

Needless to say, she ruled herself out of the puddings, but we pressed on regardless – creamy vanilla rice pudding with baked plums on the side for me and chocolate brûlée with Baileys and shortbread for my other half. The rice pudding was simply delightful and my wife's brûlée was elegance itself served in two tall, thin glasses.

As we were preparing to leave, my wife said: "Everything was just perfect."

I couldn't agree more.

Quality of Food	5
Menu Choice	4
Surroundings	4
Location	3
Service	5
Value for Money	5
Total [out of 30]	**26**

Café Coast
Beach Boulevard, Aberdeen

telephone: 01224 594488   website: www.cafecoast.com

"Food with a social conscience"

It is never easy to get things right in opening week, and it is perhaps unfair on an establishment to put it to the test so early in its life.

However, the people behind **Café Coast** in Aberdeen have had a few months to hone their culinary skills during daytime hours, and since it is now a bistro by night, we decided to put it to the test.

This is no ordinary restaurant. **Café Coast** is a social enterprise operating from the same building as the charity which supports it.

The aptly named Inspire organisation has created a fabulous building on the city's Beach Boulevard where staff work with adults with learning disabilities to create training and employment opportunities.

There's certainly no feel of a café in the decor and the warm welcome reflected the tones of the walls and furnishings. The menu is simple, with a small selection of starters, mains and desserts supplemented by a couple of daily specials.

We settled in and received our first surprise of the evening – a complimentary bottle of house wine being offered to all diners in the opening week. Having opted for white, we sipped a glass of the pleasantly fruity Australian wine

7

while making our selections.

The starter selection was limited, but it wasn't this that prompted a decision to skip the opening course and move straight to the mains. You'll discover why later.

Eating as a family, we were slightly disappointed to discover there was no children's menu and no option for half portions. They did offer us the option to select from the lunch menu for the younger diners, but it was populated with the reformed and strangely shaped food which is so often served up. This was politely declined in favour of the grown-up menu.

Our choices were poppy seed-coated fillet of pork with pearls of black pudding and glazed cider apples served with Lyonnaise potatoes, mange tout and baby carrots; grilled fillet of salmon with citrus butter-coated asparagus spears, crushed pesto, new potatoes and a summer salad; sirloin steak with chips and garnish, and from the specials, chicken stuffed with cherry tomatoes and mozzarella and served on a bed of spaghetti with pesto.

The younger members of the party were well pleased with their steak and special chicken, although the sirloin was the wrong side of medium. It was no less tasty for that, while the chicken dish was a suitably summery offering for the sunny spring evening. The meat

was cooked on the bone to ensure that it stayed moist and succulent.

The pork dish, my own choice, was superb. I don't often use such superlatives, but the blend of flavours, the tender meat and the presentation added up to one of the best dishes I've had the pleasure of eating for some time.

The salmon ordered by my wife was exactly the sort of food many chefs, Gordon Ramsay among them, preach about – fresh, light and, above all, seasonal. It was also beautifully presented.

I mentioned earlier there was a method in the madness of passing up on the starters. It was the dessert menu – short, but very sweet, and exceptionally good value for money. We chose two of the home-made sticky banoffee pudding, one shortbread tower and a Bailey's cheesecake with cappuccino ice cream.

Each was a home-made delight – shortbread with cream and fresh strawberries, light sponge with delightful toffee sauce and a cheesecake which could well be the finest I've ever tasted.

The waitress also brought us a comment card and we noted our concerns over catering for children. In fairness, if they're old enough to tackle an adult portion then the pricing makes this a viable option, but we made our feelings known just the same.

But it would be wholly unjust

to end on a negative note, however minor the gripe may sound.

If **Café Coast** can maintain the high standards it has set in its short life then Aberdeen has a new star in the making on the eating-out circuit.

Quality of Food	5
Menu Choice	5
Surroundings	5
Location	4
Service	3
Value for Money	5
Total *[out of 30]*	**27**

Café Montmartre

58-60 Justice Mill Lane, Aberdeen

telephone: 01224 584599   website: www.cafe-montmartre.co.uk

"French flavours to savour"

According to a recent survey, the UK offers among the lowest quality of life in Europe despite residents earning the highest incomes.

The price of fuel and other essential goods, below average spending on health and education, short holidays and late retirement place the UK just above Ireland at the bottom of the European quality of life index.

The weather adds to the grim tally, and I have to admit my joie de vivre has been faltering of late.

France is miles above us in the league, beaten only by Spain as the best place to live, so I wondered if catching the Gallic vibe was the key to cheering up our summer.

Swept along by this thought, we sashayed in the direction of **Café Montmartre**, on Aberdeen's Justice Mill Lane.

We walked in and it was as if we'd just strolled in off the Champs-Elysées, such is the authenticity of the restaurant. The whitewashed walls, wooden floor and timber rafters give a traditional café feel, smartened up with the white tablecloths and immaculate settings, and we immediately felt the warm glow of a French welcome.

This could have had something to do with the co-ordinated little black dresses and torturous high heels – Aberdeen gets a lot more dressed up for dinner these days – but we were charmed by the proprietor who was so archetypally French he very nearly kissed our hands.

The menu was traditional, with much meat and many wines. The amount of choice was perfect, and we were in heaven, with onion soup, tomato and goat's cheese salad, moules marinière, foie gras pâté and oven-baked snails to mull over, and that was just for starters.

I went for the spinach crepes, baked in a béchamel sauce which arrived piping hot at the table as a very generous portion. At various points through polishing it all off, I did consider leaving some room for the delights to come, but it was all so delicious that before I knew it there was an empty plate in front of me.

The crevettes across from me were wallowing on a bed of spinach in garlic and butter herbs and suffered a similar fate as they disappeared and were also declared delicious.

At this point, our patron had seen our wine choice and came over to remonstrate. Ah no, what were we thinking of with the Côtes du Rhône, he gently tutted. Deftly guiding us towards a more suitable choice, the Fleurie, a lighter red, he assured us this would complement our excellent food choices.

By now we were simpering like proper Carla Brunis, as he indulged us and complimented us in such a charming manner it was impossible to resist. And of course he was absolutely right about the wine.

The main courses were all suitably buttery, creamy and immaculately French. There was chicken stuffed with crab, the night's special was salmon and mussels in a creamy saffron sauce, there was lamb, and Normandy pork with apple, cider and cream. An entire page was devoted to cous cous, which gave a little more choice for anyone less staunchly carnivorous, but really, why would you want to stray from the traditional cuisine of the country that gave us fine dining?

I chose the duck in an orange and port sauce. By this time we were ordering in French, much to the delight of our host. There is every possibility he was also chuckling at the poor foolish Scottish ladies, but we preferred to think he was dazzled by our mastery of the language. Or the words canard and filet mignon, at least.

When my duck arrived, it was beautiful, in every sense of the word. The presentation was superb and if anything the dish was even better. The meat slid off the bones and lay gloriously basking itself in the sweetly citrus sauce. I have rarely tasted duck that was so divinely cooked, with a crackly crisp skin. It came along with potatoes dauphinoises, and garlic-drizzled vegetables which had seen their fair share of the butter dish. I really don't think I could fault them, apart from perhaps making the first course so damned good, I was filling up fast.

The steak across from me was judged to be one of the best she'd tasted and very reasonably priced compared with some high-end competitors in the city. The accompanying French fries were suitably thin, crispy and, well, French, I suppose.

As she was waxing lyrical about her filet mignon, it gave me the ideal opportunity to peruse our fellow diners. Apart from the aforementioned smart dress code, there was a good mix of the young and old, families and couples and there were even a couple of booths for a more intimate dinner à deux. The muted music aided the atmosphere rather than drowning out conversation.

Having waited a respectable length of time, we decided to look at the desserts. The tarte du maison sounded like a wonderful confection, with pastry, and fruit and crème patisserie, but I went for the bitter dark chocolate mousse. This was the only bad decision of the evening because I was sadly disappointed. It wasn't particularly mousse-like, nor was the chocolate dark, and it involved too much sponge. I know, sponge. In a chocolate mousse. Maybe this was the bit that was supposed to make me bitter.

But the sorbets across the table were amazing. Obviously all painstakingly home-made, there was a choice of five or six, although I only got to taste two of the three on my dining companion's plate before her spoon started ricocheting off my knuckles. The lemon particularly is a national speciality and this one didn't disappoint.

So while dining out at **Café Montmartre** may not help you through the credit crunch, or make up for the dismal weather in this country, maybe taking a leaf out of our continental neighbour's book and spending some time savouring life – and their fantastic cuisine – is the way forward. Vive la France.

Quality of Food	5
Menu Choice	5
Surroundings	5
Location	4
Service	5
Value for Money	4
Total [out of 30]	**28**

Carmelite
Stirling Street, Aberdeen

telephone: 01224 589101   website: www.carmelitehotels.com

"Carmelite sure to make a splash"

"This is a bit naughty," said my wife, breathlessly, as I bounded up the bedroom stairs behind her.

Don't be alarmed, this is a restaurant review, but it all began in unexpected fashion.

We had arrived early at the new and stylish **Carmelite** boutique hotel. We had heard a lot about its

food and its eye-catching bedroom designs, especially the six top-of-the-range suites, each with its own special theme.

So we asked if we could be nosey and take a brief look at a few vacant rooms. The hotel's friendly staff were only too happy to oblige.

So instead of heading straight

into the dining-room, we went off on a detour upstairs.

We were now following eagerly in the footsteps of our guide, a young general assistant called Cameron, who made us feel at home right from the moment we stepped through the revolving door of the **Carmelite**.

Suddenly, he pushed open a door and we were entering one of the best rooms – the Cabanel Suite.

My mouth gaped open. It was the first time I had seen a hotel room with its own flight of stairs, with each step lit along the way. It was dark and it looked like we were entering a nightclub or theatre.

At the top of the staircase, a devilishly sensual theme took over as the suite opened out. Its centrepiece, right in the middle of the room, was a large and elegant bath. Yes, a bath in the bedroom. Have you ever heard of such a thing? A rather seductive, large, round bed snuggled in an intimate alcove to one side, with its own mural above, and there was a handy shower made for two just off the room.

"What's the attraction of a bath in the centre of a bedroom?" I hear you say.

Well, I'll leave that to your imagination, dear reader, but let us just say it might interest visitors with romance on their minds rather than scones and high tea.

The other suites were completely different again, but just as elegant and impressive, with themes such as antique, contemporary or Japanese, for example.

As we were led down to dinner after our brief tour, our appetite for luxury had been well and truly whetted.

From our vantage point, at a corner table by the window at one end of the dining-room, we had a sweeping view through to the elegant bar, a lounge full of cosy sofas close by and farther beyond into another room, destined to become a champagne bar, at the other end of the hotel.

It had been open for only a month after a major refurbishment and the fresh, new smell, with almost a hint of paint and varnish, was still in the air.

Formerly called the Imperial and latterly the Grampian Hotel, original 19th-century features abound, including some delightful stained-glass windows.

Cameron was on hand again to deliver the dinner menu and take our orders.

The **Carmelite** has been created with a fusion of classical and modern chic, and the same sense of style had been poured over the menu.

With top Scottish chef Bruce Sangster acting as an adviser in creating the menus, this came as little surprise. Instead of starters, mains and dessert, the menu was listed as "start, indulge and temptation".

I can assure you that we covered all three bases with gusto.

It is not every day that you see that classic breakfast dish of eggs Benedict on a dinner menu, but there it was and so I ordered it.

My wife went for a twice-baked cheese soufflé.

Both were an absolute delight. The eggs Benedict was a delicious combination of poached egg, hollandaise sauce, delicate slivers of ham and a light muffin base.

The soufflé on the other side was a beautifully light and fluffy combination which proved to be something unexpected and a real treat.

For the "indulge" section, I chose roasted lamb fillet with stovies and my wife selected roast cornfed chicken with garlic and ginger crushed potatoes.

Both were beautifully presented on large, stylish dishes. My lamb was sliced into medallion shapes and they were delicately nestling on top of a round bed of stovies.

My wife's chicken was similarly positioned on its supporting act of potatoes. Side dishes of roast vegetables and home-made chips accompanied our meal.

The lamb was particularly tender and almost melted in my mouth, but both meals were top class.

For the "temptation" stage, I chose a beautifully creamy pannacotta with berries and sauce and my wife a chocolate and pecan bread and butter pudding. The combinations worked well and were given excellent presentation. The bread and butter pudding was so good I helped my wife eat it.

Both desserts would also be perfect at bath time in the Cabanel Suite, I would say.

Our only regret was that the dining-room was very quiet throughout our visit, but once word gets round, I am sure many people will be beating a path to its door. A little gem like the **Carmelite** cannot stay a secret for long.

Quality of Food	5
Menu Choice	5
Surroundings	5
Location	4
Service	5
Value for Money	4
Total [out of 30]	**28**

Casa Gabriele

4 Bridge Street, Aberdeen

telephone: 01224 590792   website: www.casagabriele.co.uk

"Picture perfect"

I have to say, I thought it was a bit odd as we stood at the downstairs entrance to **Casa Gabriele** on a Sunday night, ringing the doorbell for someone to let us in.

We hung around for a couple of minutes, tut-tutting with impatience, until we noticed the small print under the bell.

We peered at it and then at each other. It said "deliveries only".

We tentatively touched the door with our fingertips and, Abracadabra, it opened. As we raced upstairs, loudly blaming each other for the mix-up, we saw the maître d' gazing down with a smile on her face. She must have thought this was the odd couple who had been ringing the bell for the last two minutes.

Set in a grand old building at the corner of Bridge Street and Union Street in the heart of Aberdeen, this restaurant boasts an impressive, twisting staircase which seemed to go on for ever into the dark upper regions of the building. The first-floor landing opens out straight into the restaurant itself, and a warm welcome awaits.

We were led to our table next to a window, looking down on to Union Street. It gave us a view of another grand building opposite,

15

which is now the Monkey House bar and café.

We took in our surroundings, and what a refreshing place it was. There were stylish Venetian blinds decorating the windows, large pot plants everywhere and Italian street scenes running around the walls. Pride of place went to large and colourful flower displays on the walls, which we discovered were made out of delicate, thin strips of metal.

We learned that their creator was none other than Gabriele himself, the man whose name sits above the door and who plays a major behind-the-scenes role in the kitchen.

If he was equally creative with the food, we were in for a treat, we thought.

Skipping through the menu, we saw many of the old and trusted Italian favourites, but what caught our attention were the specials of the day.

I slipped out of my seat just to check them out on a blackboard near the entrance. Suddenly, the blackboard seemed to come alive and the dishes were being boomed out in a strong Italian accent. This must be the first speaking blackboard in the country, I thought.

But it was only Gabriele, who emerged from the background and continued to reel off his specials for me in a voice as rich as an arrabiata sauce.

With that introduction, we couldn't resist. My order went in for the fish special, with pieces of monkfish, tiger prawns and mussels in a white wine and cherry tomato sauce, and garlic bread. My wife went for the huge T-bone steak with all the trimmings and we shared a dish of mixed vegetables and sauté potatoes.

The dining-room was filling up nicely and there was quite a selection of visitors from around the world – South Africans, Dutch, Norwegians and Japanese.

Our main courses arrived, served personally by Gabriele. As the man from Pisa leaned over our table, I could see he was proud of his special creations. I lingered over mine before starting as it made a spectacular picture to admire.

The dish came in a beautiful bowl, decorated with fish moulded on to the design. The presentation was excellent, with generous portions of fish, prawns and mussels. The sauce was so richly delicious that it was worth dying for. I asked for more garlic bread to dip as I couldn't get enough of it.

The T-bone opposite was a monster and cooked to perfection. We were glad we side-stepped the starters and went straight to mains. These dishes really were worthy of the name "specials".

We sensed something going on at the table with the Japanese couple next to us. They had started taking pictures of their dishes. They must have been impressed, too.

My wife and I often sample each other's food as we go along, but the couple next door had now taken things to a new level – they actually swapped dishes halfway through. I know it's nosey, but you can't help noticing, can you? I sensed the woman was staring at my magnificent dish-of-dishes, but I tried not to make eye contact in case she asked to take a picture of it – or even eat it.

We thanked the waitress and asked her to send our congratulations to Gabriele. For puddings, I had to go for my old favourite, tiramisu, while my wife chose crème caramel.

Both made for a perfect end to the meal. Mine boasted layer upon layer of sponge, cream and cocoa powder. They were delicious. We also sampled a couple of very good sweet Italian dessert wines.

Our bill came to £77. As we left, I made a point of seeking out Gabriele and shaking his hand. It just seemed the right thing to do.

Quality of Food	5
Menu Choice	5
Surroundings	5
Location	4
Service	5
Value for Money	4
Total [out of 30]	**28**

The Foyer at HMT

Rosemount Viaduct, Aberdeen

telephone: 01224 337677   website: www.foyerrestaurant.com

"Foyer takes centre stage"
It seems a star is born on the Aberdeen restaurant scene.

And, what's more, it's the offspring of an existing leading light, so I suppose it's the culinary equivalent of a Redgrave or a Fonda.

For the past nine years, the **Foyer** restaurant on Crown Street has been providing imaginative, well-presented and contemporary dishes to an appreciative audience.

Its winning formula of offering excellent food with a conscience – its profits go towards preventing and alleviating youth homelessness and unemployment – means it has become an established and well loved destination.

However, the new year brings new challenges as it takes centre stage at His Majesty's Theatre, taking over the running of the restaurant, café bar and hospitality suite at the theatre.

The bright, open space, with its modern decor and acres of glass, fits into the **Foyer** ethos seamlessly, and it does feel like a natural progression for it.

We paid the place a visit when it had been there for barely a week, but it had obviously been in rehearsal for some time as the staff put in an assured performance.

The menu was as refreshingly innovative as you would expect from its pedigree, with fresh seasonal ingredients blended into some surprising and well conceived dishes.

Now, I do have to hold my hands up at the starter, because I chose badly. Despite not being the biggest fan of the ingredients of the cumin-roasted butternut squash and pumpkin seed tart served with spinach cream cheese, for some reason, I thought that, put together, I'd love them.

You're probably sitting there thinking, "that sounds quite good, actually", and yes, you probably would have enjoyed it, but it was all a bit too healthy for me – a bit too redolent of wholefood cafés and bobbly jumpers.

But it was beautifully executed, gently warmed through and did exactly what it said on the tin. I sat and gave longing glances at the Thai fish cakes opposite me, and the hint did appear to work.

They were moist little bundles of joy, the salmon set off wonderfully by the salad laden with fresh lime, coriander and cucumber pickle.

Perhaps I should, instead, have surrendered to the carnivore in me and gone for the game terrine with juniper berries and sweet piccalilli. Ah, well, something to taste next time.

The spotlight then fell on the main courses. I ordered the roast chump of lamb and, hand on heart, I can say it was the tastiest bit of lamb I've had in ages.

It was perched atop a marvellous parsnip rosti, whose sweetness combined with a pear, apricot and chilli jam to offset the meaty juiciness of the lamb wonderfully.

The chicken supreme across from me looked equally tempting, with a smoothly subtle garlic mash, sliced black pudding and beautifully wilted rocket.

The main acts of the night were definite crowd-pleasers for us. The others sounded polished and assured, consisting of smoked haddock with a bacon and leek risotto, a beetroot frittata or a curried cauliflower, pea and potato fritter.

I believe the restaurant changes its menus quite frequently so I will have to hurry to make sure I get to sample them all.

The waiting staff were, by now, working themselves up to a frenzy as the evening performance time loomed. The restaurant was full, but everyone had to get their sweets, coffee and final account before the curtain went up.

But they didn't lose their cool, remaining professional and perfectly choreographed, everything appearing with a well rehearsed flourish.

We were in no hurry so chose to linger a little with an orange and rhubarb crème brulée and some cheese.

The sweet citrus cream was set off by the tangy stewed rhubarb underneath, although the cream and spun sugar was a little superfluous.

There was a well-chosen selection of cheese and a welcome return for the pear, apricot and chilli jam.

We were an appreciative audience and I'm sure the restaurant will be playing to full houses for some time to come. **The Foyer** at HMT can definitely take a bow.

You don't have to be a theatregoer to eat at the restaurant. **The Foyer** serves lunch and à la carte dining in the evenings.

Quality of Food	5
Menu Choice	4
Surroundings	4
Location	5
Service	5
Value for Money	4
Total *[out of 30]*	**27**

Fusion Bar and Bistro
10 North Silver Street, Aberdeen

telephone: 01224 652959   website: www.fusionbarbistro.com

"Quality in the mix at Fusion"

My wife ordered a moderately priced glass of champagne, but I told the waiter I was driving.

"No problems," he replied. "You can use our Bentley."

I had to pause for a second to take in what he had said, although

I had seen a dark, sleek Bentley lounging around aristocratically at the kerb outside when we arrived.

"Yes," he continued. "It's the owner's, but we can ferry customers home if it is required."

I wish I'd known that in advance – I would have left my car at home.

Fusion might look, from a distance, as though it is tucked away in a row of accountants' offices, but there is a rather different numbers game going on inside.

First of all, do not expect a huge menu to pore over – the number of courses has been cut to a bare minimum, with just two starters and puddings and three main courses, but with an extra "special" on offer in each section.

The restaurant has also done its numbers over its mark-up on wines, and our waiter went to great lengths to explain a system which I could not quite comprehend.

Maybe it's because I always assume I am being fleeced over the wine, whereas here they appear to be saying you do not pay extra on the mark-up if you choose a more expensive wine. This was an alien concept to me and I could not quite take it in.

Where the numbers also came in during this visit was with how quickly the restaurant filled up, even although it was Saturday night, and how plentiful the staff were.

Fusion has not been open long, but word seems to be spreading fast. It might not have a large selection of dishes, but each has quality and craftsmanship stamped through it.

On the evidence of my observations, **Fusion** is also attracting a clientele to match its trendy, chic decor. Most of the people around me seemed to be beautifully manicured, with sleek outfits and sharp hairdos to match – and that was just the men. I was glad I had not worn my jeans, as planned, but now wished I had gone for a haircut.

Fusion sits in elegant North Silver Street, just off the even more elegant Golden Square, in the heart of Aberdeen. Converted from offices, the entrance opens out into a small bar and lounge area, with the dining-room to one side. The decor and furniture are smart, modern and businesslike, which fits the location ideally.

It still had that just-opened look which attracted curious passers-by. I lost count of the number of people who stopped briefly and peered in.

The staff were friendly, well informed and very attentive. We knew as soon as we stared at the menu that the **Fusion** management were being brave and bold.

After all, with only three starters to choose from, you do not expect one of them to be frogs' legs – but there it was.

I expected my wife to run

screaming from the room but, surprisingly, she ordered a portion. I went for seared king scallops with grain mustard, potato purée and crisp pancetta.

With most cuts of meat and fish, you usually do not have to think about the shape of the creature they came from when they arrive on the plate. With frogs' legs, you are left in no doubt. Several pairs of bandy, joined-together, athletic-looking legs now had their feet up on my wife's plate opposite.

She tucked in with gusto, and I, filled with curiosity, was soon joining in to help her polish them off. I have to say, they were delicately flavoured and had the same kind of texture as chicken wings. These were Oriental frogs' legs, marinated in honey soy and ginger with black and white sesame. My scallops were also very good and a light serving made it not too heavy.

On to the mains. For me, organic poached Scottish salmon with lemon and mint couscous, cucumber threads, dill and shallot vinaigrette. It was simple and elegant all at the same time, but light and not overfilling.

For my wife, it was roast star

anise duck breast with sake braised mushrooms, soba noodles, sugar snap peas and deliciously rich ponzu sauce. This really was a juxtaposition of exciting tastes. You can see where the word, fusion, comes into it to reflect the variety of influences.

For pudding, spiced créme brulèe with coffee syrup and a delightful, creamy white chocolate cheesecake with a stem ginger-flavoured base.

Fusion is a welcome new arrival to the eating-out scene in Aberdeen and certainly takes you by surprise by offering something that is a little bit different from everything else.

As we left, the Bentley was purring outside. Maybe the champagne had gone to my wife's head, but she wanted to go home in it.

I managed to talk her out of it, but who could blame her? You can acquire a taste for this kind of thing.

Quality of Food	4
Menu Choice	4
Surroundings	5
Location	4
Service	5
Value for Money	5
Total [out of 30]	**27**

G Casino

5 Exchequer Row, Aberdeen

telephone: 01224 569830   website: <u>www.gcasino.co.uk</u>

"Good? You bet"

I could not help thinking that the young Hungarian was starting to sound like a Bond villain as he stared at me across the poker table and said: "For you, there are just two options."

Oh, dear. If this was *Casino Royale* I would hazard a guess that he meant life or death.

The dealer paused for a second before he added: "You have to raise or go all-in with that hand."

This is a pretty big decision in the white-knuckle ride that is the "No Limit Texas Hold 'Em" style of poker played here.

I was playing a few hands in the rather sumptuous surroundings of the poker room at the newly opened **G Casino**, having a master class from a charming and helpful dealer. You can enjoy free tuition in the casino before you start playing for money.

This was a restaurant review with a difference. After all, we don't normally have our photographs taken for security purposes at the entrance and have to hand in our passports for inspection. Word travels fast – they must have heard about me already.

It was even odder to pick up a form which allowed me to request that I be immediately banned from the premises before I stepped inside.

The Rank Organisation's £6million **G Casino** is trying to give the world of casinos a makeover by offering a complete night out.

You don't have to gamble at all, although they would prefer it if you did, of course.

You can simply have a drink, watch the numerous large sports screens dotted about or have a bar meal or choose à la carte. Live bands also appear on a regular basis.

But it is still a casino and you have to join, which is why proof of identity is obligatory as you enter for the first time. Safe gambling is also stressed everywhere, hence the form to voluntarily ban yourself from the casino if you have a problem, and advice on how to get help.

Some Las Vegas-style stardust has been sprinkled about here. The spacious open-plan entertainment area is full of light and colour changes, and sweeping circles and curves on the walls and ceilings.

The showpiece bar is surrounded by large, comfy sofas, but what really grabs the attention is its stunning ceiling display of thousands of small flashing, coloured lights which constantly change their pattern and movement. It's like having the world's biggest slot machine flashing above your head.

Bar meals are served all day, as well as à la carte during the evening in the restaurant. An array of hot and cold meals were on offer and drinks waiters patrolled among the tables.

You can get a fried breakfast from midnight and the late bar continues well into the early hours. Burgers, pizzas, steak and eggs, and sandwiches were among the bar meals. There were even fish-finger sandwiches with tomato ketchup.

From our table we gazed across the gaming room – the heartbeat of the whole operation. Flashing lights from rows of electronic games competed with the whirr of the roulette wheels and the flicker of cards at the tables.

I quickly realised that my poker face and moody silence, rehearsed especially for the occasion, were not working.

"The waitress won't come to take our order if you keep looking like that," my wife remarked.

I dropped the act and quickly ordered prawn and crab bisque for myself and a prawn and crayfish cocktail for my wife. My soup was a creamy delight, in a delicate terracotta colour, and bursting with taste. My wife's cocktail came with generous portions of plump prawns and buttered brown bread.

A female singer was warming up during a sound check on a stage on the other side of the bar with Take That's 'Patience' followed by

Amy Winehouse's 'Valerie'. She was competing with a pre-recorded American woman's voice around the tables who kept seductively urging players to "place your bets".

For mains, my wife chose fillet steak with the usual trimmings and a red wine sauce. She swapped the chips on offer for sautéed potatoes. I went for sea bass fillets, pan-fried with lemon butter and prawns, with crushed potatoes and vegetables.

The juicy thick steak, cooked to perfection, was going down a treat, and my sea bass fillets were a lovely mixture of crispy fried seasoning on the outer skin and tender, soft fish underneath. My only minor criticism was that the crushed potato seemed on the bland side.

We rounded off with baked cheesecake and warm apple tarte tatin with ice cream. They were so good we swapped around and sampled each other's dish.

We had not finished our drinks when we headed back to the bar. Our waitress carried them over on a tray, which we thought was a nice touch. In fact, we were struck by the friendly, attentive service from the plentiful numbers of staff. Our three-course meal from the à la carte menu, with wine, came to £74.

The dress code is smart casual and trainers are frowned upon, but we saw quite a few young men sporting trainers. Tut, tut, this will never do. They just had to be rebellious poker players, I guessed.

We had enjoyed a really different night out, with a relaxed, friendly atmosphere attracting all ages.

As we left, a group of young men seemed to be watching the band intently. Or they might have been watching *Big Fight Live* on huge screens behind the band's heads. I wouldn't like to bet which it was.

Quality of Food	4
Menu Choice	4
Surroundings	5
Location	4
Service	5
Value for Money	4
Total *[out of 30]*	**26**

Jewel in the Crown

145 Crown Street, Aberdeen

telephone: 01224 210288

"Toast of the town"

It's a cold and dreary time of year just now and the continuing grey rain is enough to dampen the spirits of even the most die-hard optimist.

One look out of my window in Aberdeen at the snowdrops struggling through convinced me that overindulgence is the key to surviving the tail end of winter.

So I summoned a friend and off we went to one of our favourite haunts, the **Jewel in the Crown**, the rightly renowned Indian restaurant on Crown Street.

It has had its troubles recently – not least the fiscal problems last

year which led to a legal bid to have it wound up – but from the smiling, warm welcome I get on every visit, you would never even suspect it.

The warm and buzzy atmosphere of people enjoying the food and the company drew us in like moths to a flickering Indian flame.

It has an upper level which we've dined in before and is a complete contrast to the traditional British Asian restaurant feel of downstairs, where we were seated on this occasion, much lighter and airier but with the same fantastic food and service.

It is also rumoured that an

extension is to open very soon as well, so there will be plenty of room for everyone to sample its delights.

Anyway, we'd just got settled into the nitty-gritty of gossip and rumour when the waiter appeared with a bottle of champagne. My first thought was we'd been rumbled and this was a somewhat unsubtle (albeit potentially highly effective) attempt at restaurant review bribery – but no. It turned out my darling boyfriend had decided that we deserved something a little bit special on our night out.

Since there have been several escapades at the **Jewel in the Crown** involving mainly large amounts of Veuve Clicquot and small amounts of curry, it was peculiarly apt and might have brought a nostalgic tear to my eye.

Or my starter had arrived by this time, so perhaps it was the spices in that. It was murg chat, which had a strong and aromatic sauce with the juiciest pieces of chicken, wonderfully hot, to get the taste buds going. A marvellous accompaniment to the fizz.

My dining companion had ordered thori pakoras – thin slices of courgette dipped in a special batter with herbs and spices. It was the first time she'd tried this delicacy and it was a bit different from your normal pakora and samosa fare.

Despite the fact it was a huge helping, it felt fairly light, but it was the accompanying sauce that really made the dish. The runny, lemony, slightly herbed mayonnaise was perfect next to the crisp batter on the outside, with the inside not at all soggy and limp.

The chefs employ traditional cooking methods, but the skill they use in blending the traditional spices into a unique combination of tastes is evident in the flavours they can conjure up.

Thali was on the cards for main course. It is eaten in India as a sort of seated buffet with everything on a plate in front of you that you could ever need or think of needing. It always makes me think of a feast fit for a king – or Raj.

This didn't disappoint. There was raita, palak, a delicious seasoned spinach dish, chicken bhuna, lamb rogan josh and fried rice. It's perfect for the indecisive among you as there's a taste of everything.

It also came with a naan which was the stuff of Indian cuisine dreams, huge and pillowy with the slight sheen of oil and a well-fired base.

OK, there were actually two naans, which was completely excessive, and we should really have taken heed when our charming waiter queried the amount we'd ordered, but we were getting in touch with our inner gluttons quite convincingly by this point.

Across from me was the murg exotica, which took up less of the table than mine, thankfully, but was no less appreciated for that. The charcoal-baked chicken was excellent – succulent and all breast meat – while the hot and sour sauce was flavour-packed without being so hot you couldn't taste it.

Surprisingly, after this spread, there was no room for any more, not even a coffee, but they were quite happy to let us sit as the restaurant slowly emptied. The service is never swift, but I like to think this is deliberate, to allow for a sense of occasion and anticipation.

To be fair, we had needed the time to mull over the menu and polish off poppadoms, mango chutney and spiced onions which had been speedily dispatched to our table when we sat down.

The finishing touch, though,

was when they packaged up the leftovers for us, possibly appalled at how much food we'd left uneaten. Darling boyfriend was going to be pleased when I got home.

This illustrates my point about the service perfectly. Nothing is too much bother, you never feel you're overlooked or forgotten about and everyone is made to feel special.

Visiting the restaurant is always a delight, and I'm glad to see that standards in the family business are still so high.

If the grey skies need chasing away, I can recommend cracking open the champagne and proposing a toast to the **Jewel in the Crown**.

Quality of Food	5
Menu Choice	5
Surroundings	4
Location	4
Service	5
Value for Money	4
Total *[out of 30]*	**27**

La Lombarda

2-8 King Street, Castlegate, Aberdeen

telephone: 01224 640916   website: www.lalombarda.co.uk

"Simply smashing"

It seems everyone wants to get into **La Lombarda** – somebody even drove a car through the front window the other week.

The signs were still there for all to see, with the frontage facing Castlegate partially boarded up and posters reassuring customers that it was business as usual.

This dramatic incident and its aftermath were obviously still big talking points among staff and clientele.

I happened to mention it to the waitress as we were being guided to our table.

Before I knew it, she had gone up a gear and was accelerating, with us in tow, straight past our table. She then performed a U-turn further along to bring us to the area where the point of impact had occurred. Here, just by a temporary wall, we got a full rundown on the crash.

They must get asked about this all the time, I thought.

Back at our table near the entrance, we admired the cosy surroundings and the collection of interesting old nicknacks decorating the walls.

There was a nice, comfortable ambience to this Italian restaurant, and many eye-catching old features, including the large arched windows

29

alongside King Street. When we arrived, quite early at 6.30pm on a Friday, virtually all the tables were taken.

As the course of the evening unfolded, we became more conscious of how popular **La Lombarda** is. We lost count of the number of people turned away at the door because it was so busy.

There must have been up to twenty disappointed would-be diners who turned on their heels and trudged out again in the couple of hours we were there.

Was this because it was so popular or because they had fewer tables due to the crash? Perhaps it was a bit of both. A tip if you fancy a visit to **La Lombarda** – you must book to avoid disappointment.

Another tip for the management – please put in a revolving door at the front. It opened and closed so often that we started to feel the chill draught from outside. I almost put on my coat, scarf and my wife's gloves for the pasta course, but thought I might look a bit odd.

Although the restaurant was very busy, we never felt neglected by the staff, which can often happen in such situations. In fact, we were amazed at how quick and attentive they were as they glided by on a regular basis to check everything was OK.

The substantial and varied menus were in our hands as soon

as we sat down, which was a nice touch, and drinks followed swiftly.

I chose salmone affumicato (smoked salmon and prawns) as my starter, while my wife went for calamari fritti, or deep-fried squid.

My starter arrived like a small mountain on my plate, such was the generosity of the portion. It was a delicious combination of prawns and salmon fused together with lettuce and tomatoes. I tucked in with gusto, but there was some envy from the other side as her dish of calamari looked somewhat lightweight by comparison. But the tasty, yet light, coating of batter and zesty chilli sauce made up for in taste what it lacked in size.

I noticed I was still munching away long after my wife had finished.

If my wife felt slightly disappointed by her starter, this feeling evaporated instantly as she clapped eyes on her main course – the superb fillet boscaiola. This fillet of steak in a rich red wine sauce was a delight from start to finish. A king among dishes, the only criticism was that they were a bit miserly with the peppers which adorned the steak. This was a minor blemish on what was an excellent dish in both taste and presentation.

I went down the traditional pasta route for my main course with penne candonese, but I made a bit of a macaroni of my order, sad to say.

I had inquired whether I could add chicken to this pasta and sauce dish and, instead of the creamy sauce on the menu, could I have something rich and spicy with tomatoes?

No problem, according to the waitress, who went away as we had not completed our selections at that stage.

By the time we ordered, a different waitress was with us. I casually asked for the chicken, but forgot about the sauce. So I got the creamy version, albeit with chicken.

Waitress one (are you still with me?) noticed my glum expression and, although it was completely my fault, she offered to take it back to the kitchen and have the other version done up. I insisted that it was no problem. She even came back a few minutes later and said the chef would be happy to change it.

I would say that was a top-class piece of work from both of them, especially when you consider how busy it was. I pressed on with the creamy pasta I didn't really want and polished off the plate nonetheless.

We finished off with a delicious sticky toffee pudding, which sat like a mini-skyscraper on the dish, and a tiramisu sponge cake you could die for.

For drinks, we had a pleasant Californian rosé and a couple of liqueur coffees.

La Lombarda likes to boast that it is known all over the world and is the oldest Italian restaurant in Britain. On this showing, it has plenty to boast about.

Quality of Food	4
Menu Choice	4
Surroundings	4
Location	4
Service	5
Value for Money	5
Total [out of 30]	**26**

La Stella

28 Adelphi, Aberdeen

telephone: 01224 211414

"La Stella, a star turn"

We were stepping into that tantalising archway which leads from bustling Union Street, Aberdeen, and into the historic small lane known as Adelphi.

The lane is home to an interesting mix of establishments, including our destination – the Mediterranean-themed restaurant, **La Stella**.

It was a cold and blustery Friday, so we were grateful to escape the weather and slip into a warm welcome at **La Stella**.

I was trying to remember some of the history of the Adelphi and its unusual name.

I read somewhere that it got its name partly from merging the family name of famous architects the Adam brothers, of the 18th century, with the word, dolphin (a classical symbol of brotherly love), but the flower, delphinium, might have played a role as well. Don't quote me, please.

As it turned out, the words, cosy or intimate, could have been coined with **La Stella** in mind.

It was small and neat, with a low ceiling, attractive pillars and a small drinks serving area. There was a cluster of tables and chairs vying with each other for every inch of space, and they gave it a distinctly continental look. Cosy depends on how close you like to be to your fellow diners and here they are packed in fairly tight.

The youthful serving staff were full of smiles and eager to please. We were guided to a small table for two in a corner.

When asked if we would like drinks while studying the menus, my wife immediately ordered two coffees.

"Well, it's cold. We need to warm up," she explained, with a shiver.

I thought it would be a novel idea to continue the theme backwards after the coffee by ordering the pudding first and then the main course, but I abandoned the idea almost as soon as I started explaining my plan to my wife.

With "specials" and à la carte menus in hand, we started to browse around the dishes. There was a clear Mediterranean, or even Middle East, feel to many of the traditional ingredients and dishes.

The restaurant filled up fast and I started to worry that the service might buckle under the strain, but nothing of it. The meals came at a good tempo throughout our stay.

From the specials starters, I chose risotto with chorizo and black pudding and melted mozzarella cheese.

My wife stuck to the à la carte with smoked salmon, crispy serrano ham, Parmesan, rocket, peppers and onions prepared in a "stack" effect.

Both starters arrived in eye-catching designer bowls. My dish was rich, tasty and warming – ideal for a cold night.

But in terms of looks, my wife's starter stole the show with its impressive "stack" – but the excellent taste combinations matched the presentation.

For mains, I chose oven-baked Rock Wolfbass in a tangy tomato sauce with Parmesan mashed potato and cherry tomatoes. My wife selected Persian lamb with plums, walnuts and pomegranate sauce, and sweet potato mash.

This Persian dish brought back memories of something very similar we had enjoyed at a little Iranian restaurant near Malaga, in Spain. The dish was called fesenjaan, we thought, and my wife was really looking forward to this pleasant surprise on the menu.

It did not disappoint her. This really was an exotic dish to savour with its highly unusual tastes – to British palates anyway. The distinctive sauce complemented the plump and generous pieces of tender lamb, and the mash was a nice contrast.

Talking of contrasts, my fish was another spectacular dish, with generous slices of soft, tender fillets resting on another tasty variation on mashed potatoes. The tangy tomato sauce brought Mediterranean zest to the dish and did not seem out of place.

As I mentioned earlier, the service was pretty quick. At one point, the starters arrived at a neighbouring table where two men had become detached from their female partners, who had nipped outside for a cigarette.

"Shall we take the starters out to them?" one joked.

That would have been quite a sight, we remarked to each other.

We rounded off the proceedings with a pleasant vanilla and nutmeg tart with ice cream, and sticky toffee pudding and ice cream.

As we left, all the other tables were full. That was no surprise – **La Stella** has star quality.

Quality of Food	5
Menu Choice	4
Surroundings	4
Location	4
Service	4
Value for Money	5
Total *[out of 30]*	**26**

Malmaison

49–53 Queens Road, Aberdeen

telephone: 01224 327370   website: www.malmaison.com

"If good food is your passion ..."
The pink-tinged, chocolate-scented hint of love was in the air and we had found the perfect place to celebrate it.

We were positively quivering

with anticipation, although this may have had quite a lot to do with visiting the latest **Malmaison** in all its resplendent glory, newly opened on Aberdeen's Queens Road.

It heralds itself as a hotel that dares to be different, and it definitely lives up to its boast.

It fairly shimmers with features, which makes it an attractive destination for a romantic assignation.

We wandered through the dark and cosy bar to the brasserie, past glass rooms crammed with bottles of whisky and over a slightly unnerving glass floor which gives you a bird's-eye view of the wine cellar.

The room you enter is just as imposing, with industrial ceilings, an entire wall of gilt mirrors and life-sized images of livestock, possibly to whet the appetite.

We were seated in a mini-booth by the endlessly charming waiter, seating us side by side – all the better to gaze adoringly into each other's eyes.

The menu was what I would call couthy with a twist, but the emphasis was definitely on Scottish fare.

Alongside the choice of Shetland salmon and monkfish, locally sourced steaks, sea bass and lobster mash and Perthshire wild mushroom and truffle risotto were such local delicacies as stovies with HP sauce, classic Cullen Skink and rowie bread and butter pudding.

They do run different menus and I was a little disconcerted to find I couldn't mix and match, especially since they all appear on the same piece of paper. I could order the soup of the day but, no, I could not order Cullen Skink if I wasn't prepared to commit to that menu. There were to be no dalliances with a bit on the side here, obviously.

Thwarted in my first choice of starter, I ordered a baby portion of stovies, which came on a wooden slab with HP sauce in a baby copper-bottomed pan. This must add to the weight of the dish and, had I not caught it when it arrived at the table, it would have ended up in my lap. But it was worth catching – the right side of warming with some hearty oatcakes on the side.

Along from me was blue cheese and walnut risotto – another virtue of the seating arrangement was that his meal was far closer to my fork – sitting in an elegant pile with the tang of blue cheese managing not to overpower the comforting tenderness of the rice.

I should address the wine list at this point: it can only be described as comprehensive. It is on the expensive side, but you are certainly spoiled for choice. With a page per country, it was reasonably easy to find a good Californian Pinot Noir to complement our main courses.

These came trotting out of the kitchen, and in my case, it was very close to the truth. I had ordered the rack of Dornoch lamb, medium rare. It wasn't quite still bleating, but could have been left a little longer by a chef obviously impatient to impress.

The Rannoch Moor venison, however, was perfectly cooked, all gamey and magnificent on its beetroot gratin.

The presentation was excellent and our side orders of mashed potatoes and cauliflower cheese came beautifully served in ideal portion sizes. The meal was, indeed, an impressive sight to behold.

Having polished it off, we sat perusing our fellow diners, who seemed to be a cosmopolitan lot. Some were obviously residents, one tackling the largest burger I have ever seen, but there was a fair sprinkling of larger parties. None of this intruded, however, and **Malmaison** seems to have the ambience of relaxed dining down pat already.

We were distracted by the arrival of the rowie bread and butter pudding. This really was something else.

I realise it sounds a little gimmicky, but it was everything a bread and butter pudding should be: crisp on top, but with doughy, fudgy layers underneath, the marmalade mascarpone on top finishing it off marvellously. They sure can do their puddings.

I was suffering dessert envy, ruefully thinking of the jam sponge, mocha mousse or wild berry Pavlova that could have been gracing the table. A very decent cheeseboard consoled me no end, however, with a good selection and some very fine grape chutney.

There was a slight mix-up with the bill, where they managed to overcharge us for the food but compensated by missing our bottle of wine completely. I became a little confused, but I believe the bill, including – or maybe excluding – wine and a couple of gin and tonics, came to £86.51.

But it was a confident showing. I thoroughly enjoyed our visit and I will be back. They definitely dare to be different and, judging from the bookings they have enjoyed so far, I think Aberdeen is falling a little bit in love with **Malmaison**.

Quality of Food	4
Menu Choice	4
Surroundings	5
Location	5
Service	4
Value for Money	3
Total (out of 30)	**25**

Mim

13 Crown Street, Aberdeen

telephone: 01224 583866   website: www.mimlounge.com

"Chill-out time"

There was an almost audible frisson of excitement when it emerged one of the north-east's best-loved Indian restaurants, the Jewel in the Crown, was opening a new venture in Aberdeen.

It was being talked about as an Indian-style tapas bar, interestingly named **Mim** (pronounced meem), which apparently is the 24th letter of the Arabic alphabet, and means relax or chill. So far all the signs were looking good.

Curiosity quickly got the better of us and my friend and I waltzed into **Mim** a mere couple of weeks after it opened its doors in a prime city centre location at the top of Crown Street – close to the action but just slightly tucked back from the melee.

While word of mouth did not quite reach the crescendo of interest being generated by the Malmaison being finished just along the road, it was still pretty impressive.

With the buzz of the new venture and rumours of twenty-four cocktails on the menu, we were in a state of some anticipation by the time we headed off, and we took a break in the rain as an omen. After all, frizzy hair has ruined many a good night out.

The warmest of welcomes

greeted us as we walked through the comfy seats and sofas in the front lounge bar area and into the lounge restaurant – lounging is a feature of **Mim** with a third distinct area that looks perfect for groups to sip cocktails and graze their way through the menu.

The decor could best be described as a blend of modern Indo-Chinese, easy on the eye and appealing to a broad cross-section of the discerning city clientele.

We were given a choice of tables so took advantage to wander right through and check out the other diners – a group of oil company execs playing Blackberry fast draw, women in need of a seat after late-night shopping and the guys from the designer clothes shop round the corner checking out the talent, the usual one might say for Aberdeen on a Thursday night.

Shabbi the manager eventually left us after making sure we were properly settled in and happy with our choice of location, though he was probably quite glad to go off and attend to the friction burns on his fingers received after offering up cocktail menus.

And before anyone thinks we were overly preoccupied with a certain element of our dining experience in these times of frugality and alcohol consumption warnings, it is a tradition and we always stick to just the one

each. Well, almost always.

First things first, the cocktail list is split into three sections of eight – one for **Mim's** signature offerings (white orchids and vanilla and coconut lassis among them), one for drinks created by famous bartenders and eight synonymous with cities around the world (no prizes for guessing which is linked with mojitos and daiquiris).

So we only need to visit a dozen times to sample the entire list while drinking safely, as long as we were prepared to let the other have a tasting sip.

We finally settled on a gin-laden Ding Ho for me and an exquisite daiquiri for my glamorous companion before we eventually turned our attention to the food menu.

This came as a little bit of a surprise, and not an unpleasant one, as it explored far beyond the realms of Indian cuisine.

With a light bites section starring mini poppadoms, calamari, Thai chicken skewers and mini burgers and chips, it would be entirely possible to go for a round-the-world tapas/mezze-style experience.

But with mains such as noodle bowls, curry and rice plates, Moroccan specialities like lamb tajine, Italian dishes and even fish and chips, we went into overload.

What would we do? Go by

country theme, have a few small dishes and share, or finish our cocktails and wait for inspiration?

Not being big on the whole sharing ethos, we chose carefully to encompass a wide selection of what was on offer. All in your best interests, obviously.

My starter of salmon sushi was a beautifully presented row of three rolls served with the hottest wasabi I've ever had. But my partner-in-crime's potato cakes with tangy chickpeas won round one.

Bearing in mind the Jewel in the Crown's reputation, it was hard to bypass the tandoor section, so after a little rest I had the surkh lal chicken – tandoori chicken – and my friend had the ajwani king prawn.

This time we had a tie on our hands. My chicken was incredibly succulent and perfectly cooked while the prawns looked like squat lobster and three of them managed to fill the plate quite adequately.

But being the girls about town we are, there was something lacking, and that space in our lives was filled by a side order of **Mim** chips.

On to pudding and a slight disappointment crept in with the chocolate fondue and **Mim** doughnuts across the table, as there were too few doughnuts for the vast quantity of sauce languishing in what could have passed for a soup bowl.

At my side, the spiced pear was rather average but the coconut ice cream saved the day.

Mim is well worth a visit as a great venue to eat, drink and chill, just as it bills itself, either as a stop-off on a night out or as the main attraction.

The service was attentive without being irritating, the background music was just that and allowed us to chat without having to raise our dulcet tones and it's within a stiletto throw of a decent array of bars and clubs.

Quality of Food	4
Menu Choice	5
Surroundings	4
Location	4
Service	5
Value for Money	4
Total *[out of 30]*	**26**

Musa Art and Music Café

33 Exchange Street, Aberdeen

telephone 01224 571771   website: www.musaartcafe.com

"Top banana"

When is a banana not a banana? When it's a restaurant, of course. Musa is the species name for the banana plant. It is also the eye-catching name for the **Musa Art and Music Café**, which has taken up residence in a former Catholic church built in 1880 and latterly used as a banana-ripening warehouse by a firm of fruiterers.

I had seen an old picture from its fruit-firm days with a sign which read "Banana Department" on the front wall. Now, I mused, that could be a cracking name for a restaurant, or maybe just "The Banana House". Yes, you might say, you can see why I am not in the restaurant business.

The former church, with its distinctive rose-shaped windows at each gable and coloured side windows, sits in Exchange Street, off Guild Street, Aberdeen, close to the railway station and harbour.

It is a neglected area, yet full of historically interesting architecture which has been getting a fresh lease of life recently with new businesses moving in.

Musa had been open for ten days when we visited for dinner on a Saturday night and we could feel the tension and excitement all around.

Jens Feld, the German head chef,

was already waving a ladle at me and I had only just sat down.

He has worked previously at a Gordon Ramsay establishment, so I was slightly apprehensive over what he might do next.

It was all in good fun, of course, as the smiling Jens had overheard me asking a waitress about him and his impressive CV.

The restaurant is split between two floors, with a small, cosy dining-room on the ground floor and an upper balcony hosting comfy chairs and a small gallery.

Art and music get equal billing with the food here; an array of artwork for sale, including paintings, ceramics and hand-made jewellery, adorned the walls and display areas on both floors, while a pianist provided a relaxing classical repertoire from a small stage in a corner.

But our eyes were drawn to the open kitchen, where Jens and sous chef Dave More prowled around like a pair of caged big cats eager to spring into action.

Our table was about 12ft from the kitchen, so we could get a close-up view of these two artists at work.

Open kitchens can still suffer from an invisible barrier between diners and staff, but here Jens was building a nice rapport with guests.

From time to time, he even inquired as to how we were enjoying our food, usually from behind a cloud of steam. He also took time to show a diner a close-up view of a bream from his cold store so the guest could decide whether to order it or not.

The staff were bursting at the seams to please and make a success of the new venture.

The dinner menu was of modest size, but packed with an interesting selection of classy dishes.

For starters, we went for chickpea and coriander falafel with home-made pizza bread and marinated olives, and black pudding and ham hock spring rolls with sauce bearnaise. Both came with finely chopped salad and baby green leaves and were attractively displayed on the plate.

The small spring rolls were nice and crunchy on the outside, contrasting with a wonderfully smooth filling. The deliciously light falafel also combined nicely with the richly marinated olives and crispy pizza bread.

An impressive introduction, we both agreed.

For mains, I chose oven-baked sea bream with sautèed courgettes and mushrooms, new potatoes and red pepper pesto, while my wife opted for one of the night's specials – slow braised pork belly with an exotic star anise and gooseberry sauce.

My bream was a magnificent specimen, stretched out across

the plate with its tail and nose just dipping over the edges.

The plump and tender flesh just fell off the bone. Its clean, light taste was complemented by the richer contrasts of the accompanying vegetables.

My wife, not a great lover of pork dishes as a rule, but whose defences were lowered by the mouth-watering description, began somewhat tentatively, but was soon won over by Jens's marvellous creation. The unusual sauce combination, with its hints from the East, worked a treat. It had a savoury richness and delicate sweetness about it which had my wife singing its praises.

For puddings, we went for a pink grapefruit and ginger crème brulée with mint pesto and a warm apple tart with ginger custard and iced apple sherbert.

As with all which had gone before, both were presented with style and the entertaining combinations were cleverly worked out.

For all its obvious artistic attractions, my gaze kept being drawn to the beautiful, original wooden herring-bone high ceiling retained from the church. That stole the show for me.

Musa is an unusual dish for Aberdeen – a fusion of restaurant, café, art gallery and live music venue. The clientele was just as varied, with all ages represented, and they created a warm and friendly atmosphere on what turned out to be a busy night.

You must give **Musa** a try – you would be bananas not to.

Quality of Food	5
Menu Choice	5
Surroundings	5
Location	3
Service	4
Value for Money	5
Total [out of 30]	**27**

The Nazma Tandoori

62 Bridge Street, Aberdeen

telephone: 01224 211296   website: www.nazmatandoori.co.uk

"Nazma curries favour with my vote"

Awards, plaudits, accolades and general back-patting – that's what we all crave.

What's the point in doing something well if nobody notices?

Which is why the **Nazma Tandoori** in Aberdeen must be quite pleased with itself and its nomination for top UK restaurant in the British Curry Awards this year.

The golden envelope with the results isn't opened until the doubtless glittering awards ceremony at the Grosvenor House Hotel in London, but in the meantime I thought we'd go along and see what all the fuss is about.

Upon sharing this thought with my long-suffering dining partner, he promptly announced that scientific evidence from the Rowett Research Institute in Aberdeen has recently shown curry to be a better cure for headaches than aspirin.

He gave me a meaningful look as he said this but I chose to ignore it as I rang to make our booking.

So it was we ventured up the stairs of their Bridge Street restaurant on a Saturday night.

The Nazma has a good reputation in the city, with sister restaurants in Peterhead and

43

Inverurie and takeaways in Dyce and Banff, and I have to say the reputation is pretty well-deserved. The place was going like a fair but the well-rehearsed polite dances of the extremely professional waiters made it all seem under control despite the high turnover of tables.

You'd be forgiven for not noticing any of this going on though, due to having your nose buried in the menu. It is one of the most extensive Indian menus I have ever seen. It picks and chooses the best from throughout the sub-continent, from Kashmir and Utter Pradesh down to Kerala and Ceylon, or modern day Sri Lanka.

The ringing endorsements printed inside the menu from the likes of S Club Juniors are slightly bizarre, but hey, I've taken recommendations from stranger people in the past. Who's to say a bunch of warbling pre-teens don't know their curries from their ringtones?

They apparently do, as absolutely everything that was laid down before us was obviously freshly prepared, from the poppadoms with amazing accompaniments – which we poured down our throats and accidentally over the table while we perused the menu – to the rice and curry when it appeared.

And while I'm on the subject, why is it that I can be perfectly civilised company in any kind of restaurant, knowing what cutlery to use, the correct glass to pick up and how to attract the waiter's attention demurely, but the minute I sit down in an Indian restaurant, there's rice everywhere, spilled condiments and various sauce stains marking my progress through the meal to the extent that wearing white is an absolute no-no? It must bring out the inner glutton in me.

On this occasion, I opted for aloo dom, which is a delicious combination of potato, cumin seeds and coriander, all enclosed in a spicy batter.

Mixed pakora was across from me and although I personally find something inherently wrong with fish pakora, he pronounced it fantastic and quickly polished it off.

We proceeded on to main courses, where I'd gone for the South Indian garlic chilli chicken while my companion chose from the chef's specials with the karahi akbori.

I was interested to hear his response following the headache comments of earlier and he was certainly chomping on the chillis with aplomb. His curry consisted of chicken, lamb and king prawns, all cooked together with garlic, fresh ginger, green chilli and coriander in a spiced, creamy, buttery sauce.

It did look, and smell, very good but while curry may help sore heads it did nothing for the pain in my hand as he spiked me with his fork in order to fend off my wandering spoon.

I should have just stuck to mine as it really was good. The chicken wasn't as white and melt-in-the-mouth as I always harp on about but the dish itself was excellent with the tender spices and tomatoes mixing with the gooey garlic melting into the sauce.

Following this sumptuous feast, which was accompanied by a rather fine keema naan, ordered when I found out the fork man had never encountered one before, it was pleasant to wipe your hands, sigh and sit back, enjoying the orange slices to refresh your taste buds. Which is why there was no need for the dessert which followed.

Sticky toffee pudding was on the menu so that kept him quiet while I settled for a pistachio kulfi, followed by a black coffee served in one of their trademark mini coffee pots hovering over a flame.

The **Nazma** still has some of the slightly less than authentic hangovers from Scottish Indian restaurants. I don't believe side

salads of iceberg lettuce and tomato are indigenous to India although the swaying palms, crazy lighting and stampeding elephant motif are perhaps more in keeping with the spirit of the country.

It's a classic Indian restaurant that serves mighty fine food and we had a tremendous evening there. I wish the **Nazma** every success in the awards. They may have beaten 13,000 competitors to be named runner-up last year, but this year they seem to be on course for the top spot.

From winning the British Curry Awards in 2006 and 2007, to the Master Chef award in 2007 and, for four consecutive years, the Quality Food Online Awards, the **Nazma** comes highly recommended by those who demand something remarkable from their food.

Quality of Food	5
Menu Choice	5
Surroundings	4
Location	4
Service	4
Value for Money	4
Total [out of 30]	**26**

Number 1 Restaurant Bar Brasserie

1 Queen's Terrace, Aberdeen

telephone: 01224 611909   website: www.number1restaurant.co.uk

"And at Number 1 . . ."

A leisurely lunch has become the stuff of dreams over recent years. Precious few have the time to while away an hour or two in the company of good food, friends and wine – a quick sandwich at the desk followed by an afternoon of indigestion is the norm for most.

Sounds familiar, does it not? Which is why we were surprised during a recent trip to one of Aberdeen's newest restaurants to discover the place was packed. On a Monday. With the clock not yet striking half past midday.

Precious few places can boast that level of custom by the end of the week, let alone the beginning.

Number 1 Bar Brasserie, in the city's Queen's Terrace, is in the heart of the west-end office district, and there are clearly a large number of folks around the area who have decided that reaching for the Rennie on a regular basis is no longer acceptable.

We had wandered in on a rare day off together, and within fifteen minutes were glad we had decided to eat early. By the end of the meal, I am delighted to say our feelings had not been altered by the food or the service on offer.

Tucked away in a basement, this modern eating house and bar is light and airy despite its below street level location. This is partly down to the use of natural materials and neutral colours, but mostly thanks to a large, modern glass conservatory attached to the rear of the building and reached by an open staircase. One might say it's a building which works at all levels.

The menu is short and seasonal, but extended by a selection of daily specials. On the day of our visit, the chicken in a white wine and tarragon sauce topped with puff pastry sold out within twenty minutes of our arrival – a clear sign it wasn't something dug out of the freezer to bulk up the choices.

As we sipped our respective glasses of red and white wine, selected from a choice of two house varieties from each hue of grape, we admired the fabulous vessels from the upmarket Villeroy and Boch range – closer inspection revealed the cutlery and crockery were also of the same origin.

The question was: would the food match up to the quality of the surroundings and the hardware?

Our starters were a mixture – one from the daily special and another from the menu, a theme we stuck with for the mains. More of that later.

My honey-glazed goat's cheese bruschetta was light and packed with flavour, while the cheese, smoked bacon and olive tartlet across the table also won praise for its taste and texture.

The main courses arrived with a suitable time gap to allow proper digestion. The regular menu selection was braised beef, potato and pearl barley stew with rosemary dumplings, and it turned out to be a proper winter warmer. The ingredients blended well, although the dumplings were on the dry side.

My own special – pork and mustard sausages with a red onion mash and red wine gravy, was a variation on a British classic. The presentation was excellent and backed up by three of the best sausages I have ever tasted.

We decided to pass on the puddings, lingering instead over the last drops of wine and reflecting on a thoroughly enjoyable lunch.

Number 1 may be a relative newcomer to the culinary scene in the north-east, but with its central location, simple but effective menu and efficient service from the youthful staff, it should cement its place as one of the top spots to eat out.

Booking may be wise, though. If it can be all but full on a Monday lunchtime, one suspects it might be a hot ticket on a weekend evening.

Quality of Food	4
Menu Choice	4
Surroundings	5
Location	5
Service	4
Value for Money	4
Total *[out of 30]*	**26**

Patio Hotel

Beach Boulevard, Aberdeen

telephone: 01224 633339   website: <u>www.hilton.co.uk/aberdeen city</u>

"Representing the UK . . ."

I thought I had a touch of sunstroke after spending all afternoon in the garden on a rare hot day between the recent downpours.

We were milling around in the eye-catching, open-plan atrium area of the **Patio Hotel** with a large group of fellow diners who were also waiting for the restaurant to open.

"I know I'm not well because I cannot quite pick up what people are saying around me," I whispered to my wife.

"That's because they are all German," she replied.

She was right. We had somehow joined a coach party which had returned from viewing the sights.

Before we knew what was happening the German tourists were on the move, filing at a brisk step in neat ranks of two through the restaurant, with us caught up in the middle of the column, trying to keep pace.

I know it's a bit of a stereotype, but you have to hand it to our German friends for their swift and efficient takeover of the conservatory section of the restaurant.

We managed to avoid inadvertently spending a night

with fifty or so German tourists, although it would have been fun as they seemed a nice crowd, by baling out into the arms of the waiting staff half-way through the restaurant, who redirected us to a cosy little corner on our own.

"You've not seen anything yet," one of the waiters confided in me. "We've got fifty Italians coming in next."

I began to panic. If there were 100 ravenous tourists to be fed, where would we come on the serving list – 101st? Should we book an overnight room just in case of a long wait? Not at all, we were assured. Apparently, different teams in the kitchen were looking after the tour parties, who were having a hot buffet, and people like us who were dining à la carte.

I have to say I was a little apprehensive as we approached the hotel along the Beach Boulevard. **The Patio**, which sits opposite a fun fair and close to the beach, did not look very impressive to us. It reminded us of an oil company office block which had been deserted for the weekend.

The contrast inside could not have been greater, though. It opened out into the delightful atrium with the centre section soaring upwards and windows on all four sides looking down.

Bar and lounge merged, with menus dotted about offering reasonably-priced bar meals and snacks.

The spacious and attractive dining room opened out to the left. All the tables were dressed in elegant, crisp linen.

For starters I chose tower of sea bass, with parmesan and cracked pepper sweet tuille biscuit and roasted pepper froth, while my other half went for carpaccio of beef teriyaki, with bean sprout and red onion salad, drizzled stem ginger and chilli pepper oil.

For mains I chose a meat-lover's delight – a trio of Scottish beef. The waitress warned me it was big. In fact, she used the method employed by anglers when they boast about a catch. She spread her hands out wide and then placed them on the table to give an idea of how big it was. I got the impression she had done this a few times before. My wife went for local loin of lamb, with wild mushroom and pearl barley risotto, topped with mint farce stuffing and light rosemary jus.

The starters arrived and what a way to begin the meal. The teriyaki beef strips were displayed in a star shape and were going down a treat.

When I asked my wife if she was enjoying it, she simply replied: "I can't describe it, it's just wonderful."

My sea bass, arranged in a tower shape, was also a delight.

For mains, the waitress was right. A huge rectangular plate was laid before me with portions of meat occupying each corner. There were ribs, a 4oz fillet of beef and a braised flank of beef.

The centre of the plate was occupied by Dauphinoise potatoes, carrot puree and a beef jus to round things off.

This was a mouth-watering treat, with tender and juicy meat contrasting nicely with the delicate potatoes. My wife's lamb also proved an excellent choice, with the pearl barley and mushroom risotto a nice combination.

I have to make special mention of the staff here. They made us feel very welcome and obviously took pride in their work. At one point, one of them said: "Chef would like you to try this and let him know what you think."

It was as though we were old friends.

We were presented with what looked like ice cream cornets. A sweet and tasty pastry cone was filled with cream cheese and topped with salmon. They went down a treat, too.

A fruit pavlova with Chantilly cream and a Swiss chocolate cheesecake rounded off an excellent meal.

We spied our German fellow diners lining up for their hot buffet. I was impressed by their discipline and queuing technique. We British like a good queue, but if there was

a world queuing championships, I think they would beat us.

There was a hubbub nearby and we realised the Italians had arrived. Now their grand entrance was somewhat different. They simply swarmed all over the place in typically relaxed Mediterranean style.

Their queuing technique left something to be desired, though. Tut-tut.

Joking aside, I have to say that all of our international contingent were a charming and polite bunch.

We wondered what it would be like if a coach party of Brits turned up next.

"Anarchy, probably," I joked.

There were more than 100 people sitting down to eat, but it did not feel crammed and neither did the service suffer.

It turned out to be something of a *Eurovision* evening, but I would be happy to sing **The Patio's** praises in any language.

Quality of Food	5
Menu Choice	5
Surroundings	4
Location	4
Service	5
Value for Money	5
Total [out of 30]	**28**

The Patio Hotel was taken over by Double Tree at Hilton in September 2008.

Pavarotti's

27 Union Terrace, Aberdeen

telephone: 01224 622555

"Pavarotti's double act"

I felt a nudge on my shoulder followed by the excited voice of Mario, the manager: "There he is, the best chef in the world!"

And, sure enough, there he was. Peering out from around his kitchen door, resplendent in his whites with curly, black hair spilling out from under his hat was Carlo, from Rome.

I don't know for a fact whether he is the best chef in the world, of course, but Mario seemed convinced that he was. And I had asked about the chef in the first place, which is why Mario brought it up.

Mario was not slow to sing his praises but, let's face it, we are talking about Italians and Italian food. They have plenty to be proud of and to boast about when it comes to food and culture.

Napoli-born Mario had firm views about the best place in Italy to visit and it began with an "N" funnily enough but, despite that, he and his Roman chef made an irresistible combination.

They need to be larger than life with a restaurant called **Pavarotti's**, after all.

It sits in elegant Union Terrace, Aberdeen, opposite the pretty Union Terrace gardens and close to the HM Theatre.

Not surprisingly, **Pavarotti's** is popular with theatre-goers and has a pre-theatre menu from 5.30pm to 6.30pm, Monday to Saturday.

Possibly for that reason, the restaurant had the hustle and bustle of a place where things happened quickly and there was a lot of coming and going.

I, personally, prefer that to the long, lingering meal which drags on for a slow-baked eternity. Why linger when you've eaten, I always think.

For example, at **Pavarotti's** we had ordered, eaten our starter and were beginning our main course after just half an hour. That's my type of place.

We had booked the day before – a wise precaution as people were being turned away on the Friday night we visited.

On arriving, we spied a nice window seat, but were politely declined the option by you-know-who, as it was already reserved.

We ended up tucked away on a table for two, sandwiched between a pillar and the drinks service counter. This also seemed to be the marshalling area for Mario and his team of energetic, friendly staff.

We feared we had landed between a rock and a hard place, a culinary version of Piccadilly station and a rather busy junction in the restaurant.

We were alongside the main line between the tables and the kitchen,

but the flurry of activity around us turned out to be great fun.

Mario was like a station master, directing the staff in and out of tables, with "number five ready to depart and number six about to arrive".

The staff were busy, yet always eager to please. Mario, for example, took time to study the little map on the back of our Italian bottle of rosé after I spotted that it came from the vineyards around Acquaviva. I said I thought I had been there and wondered whether it was the actual vineyard I had visited at the time. Waiting staff have to have the patience of saints, don't you think?

Our starters arrived in a flash. I went for grilled vegetables stuffed with Parma ham, flakes of parmesan cheese and salad.

My wife chose crispy fried squid and courgettes on a bed of raddachio leaves.

Both were beautifully presented and were light, yet delicious combinations.

The à la carte menu at **Pavarotti's** offers a good variety of dishes, yet contains quite a few surprises. This is not the sort of place you come to for wall to wall pasta.

For mains, I chose bite-sized portions of monkfish, sautéed in olive oil, with salad.

Again, this dish was delightful to look at and appreciate before tucking in. The fish portions were displayed in a circle around the plate. It seemed a shame to disturb them, but I just had to. The fish was superb, with the olive oil giving it a tasty and moist flavour.

My wife went for an Aberdeen Angus steak, medium rare, with large flakes of parmesan cheese, drizzled with balsamic vinegar, and salad leaves.

The steak was nicely sliced into attractive shapes. The cheese and steak combination was unusual, for us, but worked well. My wife said it was delicious, but I insisted I had to check for myself in the interests of a proper report, of course.

A special mention for Carlo's oven-baked, sliced potatoes in rosemary must be made here. We ordered them as a side dish and they were simply marvellous.

For puddings, it was a delicate and mouth-watering tiramasu and chocolate and vanilla ice cream for me.

We rounded off with an espresso coffee for me and an espresso corretto for my wife. The latter contained a generous measure of grappa Italian spirit.

It was a knockout. In fact, had she drunk a second I think it would have knocked her out.

I don't know what was showing at HMT, but Mario and Carlo make a great double act over the road.

Quality of Food	5
Menu Choice	5
Surroundings	4
Location	4
Service	4
Value for Money	4
Total [out of 30]	**26**

The Prime Cuts Steak & Lobster House

21 Crown Terrace, Aberdeen

Telephone 01224 589696   website: www.theprimecuts.co.uk

"A cut above"

It was obvious the waiting staff at **The Prime Cuts** were well drilled in the art of looking after guests.

We were twisting our necks around to admire the decor in the dining-room, which is apparently modelled on a real New York steak house.

I soon noticed that if I turned my head a fraction past 90 degrees it was classified as a nod for help and a friendly waiter was at my side.

The next time I unwittingly turned too far, I pulled a face to try to indicate I was simply admiring the decor again. I failed miserably.

They obviously thought my exaggerated face-pulling meant I was having a funny turn and two waiters turned up.

To avoid this happening all night, I began studying huge mirrors adorning one of the walls so I could check out the room through the reflection – careful, of course, not to make eye contact with the waiters in case they had the mirrors covered as well.

I knew there was something special about **The Prime Cuts** before we even sat down because it kept telling me at every opportunity.

It announced proudly on a sign

outside that it was Aberdeen's only steak and lobster restaurant. Just inside the door was a large board packed with more information, including details of a special 28-day curing process which made all the steaks, well, special.

It told us about the process and the Speyside meat supplier who played a key role in it. To cap it all, celebrity chef Antony Worrall Thompson's name appeared endorsing it.

Doors opened to reveal a large, cavernous dining-room with a familiar shape. Someone told me it used to be La Bamba restaurant, which I remember from a previous visit, which has moved a few doors along Crown Terrace.

We were a good half-hour early, yet the courteous and friendly staff were able to accommodate us in a nice corner table. Joking aside, although the staff were ultra-attentive throughout our stay, I suppose that is preferable to staff who never seem to make eye contact.

They were happy to talk through the menu and the concept of the restaurant. Not surprisingly, **The Prime Cuts**, they told us, was especially popular with American oil people. A quick scan of the menu showed it was definitely pitched upmarket.

Steak and lobster, in a variety of forms, dominated, of course, with some of the steaks hovering around the £30 mark. The steaks occupied a mini-menu all of their own within the main menu. Starting from a standard steak "special" at £15, the prices and quality steadily increased.

For starters, I chose lobster bisque and my wife a lobster cake. The latter resembled a rather large fish cake topped with sweet red-pepper chutney, which opened to reveal a deliciously fluffy and substantial lobster filling. It was a memorable dish which we had not encountered before.

My bisque boasted a heady richness that was almost overpowering. Blended from lobster shells, with oven-roasted tomato, finished with double cream and cognac, it also tasted as though the lobster had brought the sea with it, such was its distinctive, rich saltiness.

For mains, I went for a standard rib-eye steak while my wife chose one of the specially-cured centre-cut fillet steaks, "upgrading" from an 8 to 10 oz, which can be done on request. These came with a variety of vegetables, including excellent asparagus tips, and side dishes of home-made chips and sautéed potatoes.

I only discovered later that the extra two ounces on the fillet also added £8 to the bill, increasing the fillet from £22 on the menu to £30, which was more than a heavyweight 20-ounce T-bone.

My two generous slices of rib eye were fine enough, but I could not take my eyes off the fillet opposite. Eventually, my wife relented and I tried a slice. The difference in taste and texture hit me straight away – like comparing vaudeville with Broadway in this New York diner.

We rounded off with a superb baked Alaska for my wife and a baked vanilla cheesecake and ice cream for me.

I had forgotten a small note on the menu about an "optional" service charge. Maybe I mistakenly thought it would only be added at my request. Now I was too embarrassed to query it as it appeared on the bill. At £10.40, it pushed the bill to £114, including a couple of beers and two glasses of wine. A bit steep, possibly?

Some would say you have to pay for quality; others argue that as you are paying a premium price already, an "optional" service charge is unnecessary. You would then have the option to tip staff directly at your own discretion without feeling awkward.

Nonetheless, it was still a quality evening, although pushing the boat out here might require a corporate card or a special occasion. There are more economical meal variations on offer here as well, however.

Looking about, we spied a young mum and her small child admiring lobsters through a large tank near the entrance. The child was pointing excitedly, as they do while on family visits to sea aquariums. A working restaurant is something else, though. As we left, a lobster scurried nervously for cover behind a rock. It had probably been watching as we paid the bill.

Quality of Food	5
Menu Choice	5
Surroundings	4
Location	4
Service	4
Value for Money	4
Total *[out of 30]*	**26**

The Sand Dollar Café and Evening Bistro

2 Beach Esplanade, Aberdeen

telephone: 01224 572288   website: www.sanddollarcafe.com

"A seaside treasure"

I knew straight away that the **Sand Dollar** was a popular place because they wouldn't let us in.

At first, I thought they just did not like the look of me, but they said politely they were fully booked for the night. Drat! I knew we should have booked.

We hung about, looking forlorn, until the two lads running the front-of-house service took pity on us. One disappeared to talk to the chef and, hey presto, our luck was in. He came back with a smile on his face and said they could just fit us in.

A few minutes earlier, we had been strolling along the beach esplanade, taking in all the sights and sounds out to sea and around the beach on a pleasant early Saturday evening. We could almost shut our eyes and guess what particular eatery we were passing just by the aromas which were swirling around. The smell of food on the breeze was giving the bracing sea air a run for its money.

All sorts of interesting diners and cafés now pepper the beach front in the shadow of the big wheel at the fair. You could almost miss the **Sand Dollar** with its narrow frontage. Once inside, though, it opens out into a longish dining-

57

room with a warm and welcoming atmosphere.

Maybe it was the drink, but our minds began to drift as we gazed out from the **Sand Dollar** towards the sea, and it was almost as though we had been transported to somewhere exotic, like Florida or the Mediterranean.

The **Sand Dollar** has a split personality; by day, it serves the passing breakfast and lunch trade, but for a few nights a week it also offers an à la carte menu.

An interesting, but not over-elaborate, set of meal choices gave us plenty to talk about. For starters, my wife went for marinated seared king prawns on bruschetta while I chose pan-seared fresh scallops with crispy bacon, sage, puy lentils and green salad. Both these dishes looked great on the plate. They were simple, yet full of taste and colour.

For mains, my wife tried the 8oz sirloin steak while I selected the eye-catching roasted fresh monkfish wrapped in Parma ham with sun-dried tomatoes and basil and served with lemon mash and fresh vegetables.

We were really pleased with our choices. My wife's steak, with its accompaniment of chunky potato wedges, was tender and succulent.

My monkfish dish was a collision of tastes and textures which combined well, and the lemon mash was delicately flavoured rather than overpowering.

We were admiring a collection of striking paintings for sale which decorated the walls. It turned out that they were the work of a well known local artist. Our waiter then confided in us that the artist himself was sitting at the prized window table with some fellow diners. We gazed towards his group. I could not help noticing that they appeared to be quite nicely framed in the window.

We rounded off with a couple of delightful puddings – old-fashioned rhubarb trifle topped with pecan nuts and served with cream, and apple and sultana pudding served with vanilla crème fraîche. These were definitely not your run-of-the-mill desserts and made a pleasant change from the usual pudding menus we have seen elsewhere.

The restaurant was now filling up with a lot of those pre-bookings I mentioned earlier. Even so, director/chef Suzi Millard came out of the kitchen to move around the tables to talk to guests. It was obvious some were regulars, but she knew we were first-timers and made a special point of welcoming us, which I thought was a great touch.

After bidding farewell, we strolled along by the beach. In some parts of the world, you might find a sand dollar, a small marine creature related to sea urchins and starfish, wriggling about in the sand. In

America, youngsters find their discarded shells on beaches and, due to their unusual shell pattern, think they look like coins – and call them sand dollars. On this beach in Aberdeen, however, the **Sand Dollar** restaurant itself is the real find.

Quality of Food	4
Menu Choice	4
Surroundings	4
Location	5
Service	4
Value for Money	5
Total *[out of 30]*	**26**

Sopranos Wine Bar and Bistro

20/22 Guild Street, Aberdeen

telephone: 01224 589411   website: www.sopranohotels.co.uk

"Sopranos strikes the right note"

Despite the constant talk of recession, Aberdeen's harbour area is in the middle of a regeneration.

The multimillion-pound development at Union Square hopes to tempt the cosmopolitan citizens with its endless spending opportunities; the old eyesore bus station has been razed to the ground and replaced by a sleek new edifice, and the railway station is undergoing its own face-lift.

Hoping to ride on this tide of optimism in the area is **Sopranos Wine Bar and Bistro** on Guild Street, located in the St Magnus Court Hotel.

Catering to the young and affluent, it provides an informal and laid-back meeting place where you can enjoy a glass of wine, a few drinks with friends and some tapas, or something more substantial from the dinner menu.

The evening we dropped in was proof of its early success. The bar area was buzzing with bright young things with bottles of champagne chilling in ice buckets – not the usual Guild Street scene at all.

The decor is an eclectic mix of design with a green glass mosaic wall, Romanesque busts, chandeliers and an unusual wall lined with the ends of wine boxes.

It claims the concept fuses together design ideas from Florence, Sienna and Paris. I'm not sure how fused together it is, but it's delightfully different and certainly has an atmosphere of somewhere comfortable, yet suitably chic, that you would enjoy spending time in.

Unfortunately, the buzz in the bar meant we were left standing looking vacant for a bit. There was no one to find our table or even acknowledge us and we had to wait our turn at the bar to announce our arrival.

But we coped and soon we were seated in an alcove at one of the hand-carved oak tables with a menu and many people waiting on us, so we didn't feel neglected for long.

There's a great tapas selection, as well as what looked like a decent Mediterranean-style bistro lunch, but it was the dinner menu we turned to. It hovers around France, Italy and Spain with lots of fish and pasta dishes, and lots of tomato and herbs.

I passed on the fish soup and goat's cheese and swithered over snails, but eventually settled for king prawns skewered and marinated in ginger, garlic and chilli. The prawns were deliciously moist with a slight chargrilled crunch and in just the perfect portion size.

Across from me, my dining companion was tucking into Parma ham with melon and minted citrus fruit salad. The sumptuous sheets of Parma ham draped across the delicately balled melon were drizzled with a tart citrus dressing. It was quite a start and my hopes were high for the main courses.

We had gone for the sea bass and the steak, and when my companion's steak arrived I was gobsmacked by the size of it – but no less by the size of the chunky chips. They were massive. I had a perspective moment worthy of Gulliver when they were so big I thought they must be sitting on my plate and not across the table from me, but alas, no. Quite incredible.

The peppercorn sauce was spicy; it was an impressive sight

and apparently delicious, although there was a bit much blood around the medium to well-done steak to my eyes.

My sea bass was also looking good. With tomato and basil sauce sloshed over half of it, it lay on a liberal dollop of sweet potato and coriander mash – always a winning combination in my book. Beautifully prepared and presented, the mix of flavours was perfectly balanced with nothing overwhelming the fish.

The food had definitely impressed, but the service was a little less polished. Don't get me wrong, they were utterly charming. There's just a slight training issue here.

Our wine arrived, but without glasses, our main course without cutlery, and by the time dessert arrived, our aperitif olives were still sitting on the table. That said, they were solicitous and friendly, and nothing was too much trouble, but someone needs to tell them to check for side plates and napkins.

I was soon distracted by the arrival of the desserts. The plates were like mirror images of each other, each on an oblong platter with sorbet sitting in a brandy basket, but there were two completely different experiences.

Undeterred by her fiery pepper sauce, my dining companion had gone for the peppered strawberries on vanilla panna cotta with a balsamic vinegar sorbet. This was the first time I'd come across balsamic vinegar sorbet and my scepticism must have been wafting across the table because it was soon pushed in my direction and, I have to say, it was light, interesting, refreshing and perfect with the strawberries. I take it all back – a perfect end to a meal.

My amaretto and pear cheesecake had been a bit of a gamble because basically I'm not a huge fan of cheesecake. I love cake and I love cheese, so my theory goes that I'm always disappointed in my expectation of cheesecake being the best thing in the world.

However, this was creamy rather than cheesy, and the almonds in the liqueur brought out the mellow pear-ness of it all, echoed in the chunks of pear in the sorbet. None of the pepper or vinegar across from me, but very creamily seductive.

I should mention the wine list as it's one of the selling points. It is extensive and **Sopranos** sells a grand variety by the glass or by the bottle, allowing you to enjoy a bottle over dinner or a glass with a friend on a Saturday afternoon, or share a bottle after work.

And this is **Sopranos'** greatest strength. It has a flexibility and friendliness that is a winning combination. It knows where it is headed and what its customers want. The food is of the moment and, while not pushing the boundaries, that's not what it wants to do.

If you are looking for an elegant and modern destination then head for Guild Street – the cool people won't be far behind you.

Quality of Food	4
Menu Choice	5
Surroundings	5
Location	4
Service	3
Value for Money	5
Total *[out of 30]*	**26**

The Stage Door
26 North Silver Street, Aberdeen

telephone: 01224 642111

"A star performance"

I was wondering why **The Stage Door** restaurant had such a warm, relaxing feeling – it kept washing over me all through our visit.

It was so good I wanted to stretch out and stay all night.

My theory was that it had something to do with its past as a theatre and cinema.

That's it, I thought. There were so many laughs down the years that they have soaked into the walls, making it a happy place.

You might be wondering, at this stage, what I was drinking. Perhaps it was me who was getting too happy.

It was a rather pleasant rosé from Provence, actually, but I was only intoxicated by a lovely dining experience from start to finish.

We entered from elegant North Silver Street, which runs off Golden Square, and clambered up a draughty, twisting stairway that was probably not unlike many a stage door entrance in grand old theatres.

We were soon bathed in warmth and light, though, as the doors swung open at the top to reveal a large, sweeping dining area topped by a spectacular arched, Art Deco ceiling with skylights dotted about.

To the left was a section with a glass partition, which was the former smoking area, packed with diners, even although it was not yet 7pm.

These turned out to be guests taking an early theatre menu who were grouped in the same place for ease of serving, presumably. We were guided past them to the smart, spacious and lightly populated main dining area illuminated by soft lights and candles. We felt like the toffs going to the dress circle.

We were struck by how welcoming the staff were. As time drifted by, we also noted how consistently attentive and efficient they were.

We settled into a table for two which was unusually roomy, not at all like those awkward, cramped tables for two where you need to be a circus juggler to keep things from falling off.

There was a transatlantic atmosphere in the air. The background music was playing Sammy Davis Jr's classic, 'Bojangles'. Peering through a large plant between us and the next table, I could hear our dining neighbours were from Texas and the waitress taking their orders turned out to be from upstate New York. If I had craned my neck any further while eavesdropping, I would have fallen into the plant pot, so I cannot tell you any more about them, except to say that Americans do enjoy meeting each other in faraway lands.

Menus in hand, we ranged far and wide over an interesting selection. For starters, my wife chose aromatic crispy duck on a julienne of vegetables with spicy plum and ginger coulis.

I went for king prawns wrapped in Parma ham and coated in crispy batter with a chilli mayo dip.

I hoped it would come quickly as I was feeling a little peckish, but I kept thinking of a light-hearted message from head chef Alan Macdonald, written on the front of the menu, asking diners to be patient while his team created their masterpieces.

"It took Van Gogh three years to paint 'The Sunflower', but just five seconds to cut his ear off", it read.

It makes you think, does it not?

With my ear to the ground, I

could tell the starters were on their way, and they actually arrived pretty quickly.

They were presented excellently. Delicious chunks of duck on the plate opposite, surrounded by a meandering light stream of sauce, made for an unusual and delightful starter.

For me, the ham embracing the prawns and sandwiched between the batter coating were great combinations.

I asked Kate, our American waitress, to hold back on the wine until our main courses arrived. What was interesting was that after she poured our first drink, she popped back periodically to serve top-ups just when we needed them, but not in a pushy way. It was a nice touch.

For mains, my wife chose breast of chicken stuffed with ham, cheese and herbs, with a basil risotti, in a rich red wine and mushroom sauce. I went for roast chump of lamb on a potato and onion rosti, with carrot and parsnip puree and light mint jus.

My mouth is watering just writing about it, such were the powerful and lighter flavours

working superbly together. The presentation could not be faulted, either. Both were first class.

A slightly embarrassing time after ordering had elapsed when we decided we wanted a dish of garlic mushrooms as well. I feared an "ear bending" from the kitchen, but it was no trouble at all.

Apple and plum crumble with cinnamon ice cream for me and peach melba meringue and ice cream, with raspberry coulis, for my wife rounded things off. Yes, they were as good as they sound.

I must mention the waiting staff again. They never stopped working the tables in a polite and unobtrusive way, and were an object lesson on how it should be done.

So the final curtain came down on our visit to **The Stage Door**, and what a great performance it was.

Quality of Food	5
Menu Choice	5
Surroundings	4
Location	4
Service	5
Value for Money	5
Total [out of 30]	**28**

Banchory Lodge Hotel

Dee Street, Banchory

telephone: 01330 822625   website: www.banchorylodge.co.uk

"Simple Dee-lights"

There's an old charm to the **Banchory Lodge Hotel**. Tucked away from the commercial heart of Banchory, and nestling by the River Dee, this particular hostelry oozes character.

The dining room has without doubt one of the best views of any in Scotland. On a summer's evening you can watch the anglers in pursuit of the salmon and sea trout that are legendary on the Dee, or just marvel at the scenery.

If you're lucky you can also listen in on the fishy tales of the anglers as they talk over dinner, or in the bar, about the one that got away.

Years ago the hotel was the scene of an infamous fishing excursion on the Dee when an overly generous host plied my friend and his pal with too much brandy before they cast their rods at the Junction Pool. Not surprisingly, there were no fish that evening. That they didn't fall in was also a miracle.

For the last forty years the **Banchory Lodge** has been run by the Jaffrays, Margaret and her late husband, Dugald.

They took over the establishment in the swinging 1960s when my dining companion was but an over exuberant youth and who was almost ejected from the premises for firing a soda fountain at a particularly riotous stag party.

Four decades on and he was a degree more sober, although he fondly recalled the incident and numerous other parties. His tales were a delight, just as the conservation was on the neighbouring table by a group of frightfully posh folk, up for the fishing.

I shared their sentiments that MP Margaret Beckett, the UK's environment, food and rural affairs secretary, was a bounder.

Their gripe was over hunting; mine over her, and the Government's persistent lack of appreciation that Britain needs to produce its own food, rather than rely on imports from politically unstable nations who are just as likely to shut the door on sales as Russia did when it closed the main gas pipeline feeding Europe.

We started in the hotel's quaint bar, where the anglers were debating over whether it would be champers or wine with their meal. Our order was simple; two large gin and tonics and a diet Coke for my companion's long-suffering wife.

The dinner menu was simple, but effective, catering for all.

Our appetites suitably whetted we opted for the smoked fish

platter and the Mediterranean vegetable layer for starters followed by baked salmon, a sirloin steak and a fillet of chicken. I felt the need to show support for Britain's poultry industry after the TV-led media debacle in recent weeks over the discovery of bird flu in a solitary swan.

The smoked fish – salmon, trout and mackerel – ticked all the right boxes, as did my layered vegetables; grilled courgettes, tomato and red pepper wrapped in baked Parma ham and served with a mozzarella cheese.

The main courses did not disappoint either. The now sober pensioner appreciated the baked salmon served with a delicious fennel and Pernod sauce.

His wife found the sirloin steak cooked as she wanted it. Her disappointment was with the aged balsamic syrup that was served with it. My own feeling is that good beef does not need the additional jus, gravy, syrup or sauces. That merely disguises the taste of the main dish.

The presentation of my fillet of chicken was not akin to a piece of poultry. That said it was tasty, and well complemented by a slice of haggis and a whisky cream sauce.

Chicken can often be overcooked and dry, but this time it was done to perfection.

The option of dessert was taken up. A ginger sponge that went down a treat, strawberries and ice cream with one solitary raspberry in the bowl, and the cheese and biscuits. Unlike so many other establishments, the **Banchory Lodge** doesn't scrimp on the biscuits.

Our meal was washed down with a particularly delightful Spanish Rioja called El Coto. Wonderfully fruity and oh so easy to drink.

Our main gripe would be over service. The feeling was that the staff were not as attentive as they could have been.

But there were two large groups also dining and they did require attention.

Our problem was over the delay between finishing desserts and getting our coffee. Strangely too, it proved a little difficult to get the bill, but was very reasonable.

Quality of Food	4
Menu Choice	4
Surroundings	5
Location	5
Service	3
Value for Money	5
Total *[out of 30]*	**26**

Boar's Head Restaurant

Kinmuck, Inverurie, Aberdeenshire

telephone: 01224 791235   website: www.theboars-head.co.uk

"A cosy hideaway"

I looked at my wife across the dinner table and asked: "Tell me, have we entered the *Twilight Zone*?"

She paused for a second and then replied: "No, we are still in Kinmuck."

That was a relief as we had encountered an amazing coincidence. Just before we arrived at the **Boar's Head** we had been discussing what type of menu might be on offer. I thought vaguely that it had a surf and turf theme.

As we pulled into the car park we were reminiscing about our last surf and turf meal and agreed it had been at the rather exotic Zanzibar restaurant in Inverness some while ago.

As we flipped through the **Boar's Head** menu I noticed the chef's name was Stuart Walker. I asked the co-owner why this rang a bell and she said: "Oh, Stuart used to run the Zanzibar in Inverness."

Cue *Twilight Zone* music. What a happy coincidence and I knew that we were in for a treat.

Our journey to Kinmuck, nestling on a quiet Aberdeenshire back road between Hatton of Fintray and Inverurie, took place on a Friday night at the start of Easter weekend, which meant it was cold, snowing and blowing a gale.

We had not seen another car for what seemed like miles and then we discovered, as we ventured into Kinmuck with twinkling lights on the **Boar's Head** acting as our beacon, that every car in the locality appeared to be in its car park.

Getting out of our car was one thing but getting into the restaurant was something else as we were buffeted by the gales. Luckily, co-owner Jaclyn had spotted our plight as we struggled to even reach the door, let alone open it. She threw it open and more or less dragged us in.

What a haven it was inside the dining room. A cosy hideaway in traditional style, with a beautiful, original brick wall running the length of one side of the room and furnished with attractive, heavy wooden tables. A huge fireplace twinkled with a large collection of candles.

Jaclyn, twenty-six, who has recently taken over the **Boar's Head** with partner Helen, ran through the menu specials with her distinctive accent – a north-east twang fused with a Kentucky topping (courtesy of her American parentage and time at the American School).

This was anything but a surf and turf eatery, although it was on the menu. Stuart's imagination and love of experimentation had been given full rein by Jaclyn and Helen and the result was a good mix of old favourites, with a new twist, and fresh ideas.

While I plumped for Cullen skink as a starter, my wife chose Thai casserole – what a contrast. Not the sort of combination you would normally come across in a rural north-east bar/diner.

It was a perfect night for a Cullen skink and Stuart did not let me down – this really was up there with the best I had tasted. This version boasted generous portions of smoked haddock, with a lovely large chunk floating near the surface, mixed with potatoes, leek and a creamed fish fume.

From the north-east to the Far East in just the width of a table and there was my wife's Thai casserole in all its glory. This colourful and unusual dish comprised of crayfish tortellini, squid, white crab, yoghurt, pea shoots and sweet and sour sauce. It was an exotic treat.

Jaclyn kept popping through to check on us with a laugh and smile and made us feel at home. From the general hubbub in the distance from the bar, there was a happy atmosphere around the place.

For mains I went for surf and turf, with a new spin. Monk tail fillets and Arbroath smokie combined in a cream and light brown swirl, and were then encased in Parma ham to make generous parcels on the plate. Creamed tundra cabbage provided a tasty bed for the surf and turf.

This really was a delicious and eye-catching dish.

Over the way, my wife chose the beef tasting platter. This arrived on a wooden board boasting three small steaks – sirloin, fillet and rib eye. Tomatoes, mushrooms and home-made chips completed the picture. There was so much, I wondered if someone was joining us. I suspected I would be called into service to help her with this dish – and so it proved. The steaks looked small but they packed a punch. A must for meat lovers.

For puddings, for me it was a delicious lemoncella liqueur parfait, a frozen custard cream delight, with homage to Picasso as the chef decorated the plate with dramatic sauce colours, and a sherry trifle for my wife.

As we settled the bill, chef Stuart came out for a chat with us about his passion for food and to get our opinions, which I thought was a nice touch.

We moved into the friendly bar just in time to catch co-owner Helen perched on a stool in a corner, singing and playing the guitar to entertain her guests – and a very impressive performance it was, too.

The **Boar's Head** also does bar meals and Sunday roasts, but for food lovers the quality of its à la carte menu marks it out as something special – a little gem hidden away in the countryside.

We enjoyed ourselves so much, my wife said she wanted to move here. At first, I thought she was talking about Kinmuck, but she might have meant the **Boar's Head**.

Quality of Food	5
Menu Choice	4
Surroundings	4
Location	4
Service	4
Value for Money	5
Total [out of 30]	**26**

The Cock & Bull

Ellon Road, Balmedie, near Aberdeen

telephone: 01358 743249   website: www.cockandbull.co.uk

"Coming up trumps"

My old reporter skills were flooding back as I sensed I was on the brink of an exclusive.

I was flicking through the pages of the visitors' book at the entrance to the **Cock and Bull.**

I was searching for hidden gems. Yes, gems of wisdom from American billionaire and north-east golfing entrepreneur Donald Trump.

After all, he had popped into the **Cock and Bull** for dinner a week before, after surveying his proposed new golf kingdom over the road, and I was retracing the great man's footsteps.

There were names and comments about the restaurant

listed from variously exotic locations such as Norway, Arkansas and Ellon, and even someone who said they could not remember where they came from. They must have had a good night.

Alas, the one I really wanted to see – signed "Mr D. Trump, of Trump Towers, New York" – was nowhere to be seen, as far as I could tell.

Aw, shucks. I would just have to see if there were any clues to his visit inside.

It had been a long time since I was last at the **Cock and Bull**, a delightfully elegant cottage-style restaurant just a few miles north of Aberdeen.

A warm and friendly welcome awaits you; it is the sort of place where you want to linger and relax. It also boasted two chefs in the running for the Grampian chef of the year awards.

It is stacked to the gunnels with antique-style bric-a-brac and collectables. It is like a cross between a grand old country home and an Aladdin's cave of interesting objects.

There are several dining areas in various nooks and crannies and a newer conservatory at the rear. We were guided into an elegant room to the left and settled into a cosy little corner.

I was sandwiched between a shelf sporting an original Singer sewing machine and a classic old camera (both very collectable, I believe) and a wonderful display of old hats decorating a stand.

To one side of us was a family group of about ten, including a charming little girl who kept wandering about and blowing a paper trumpet when you least expected it.

As our waitress arrived with the menus, I slipped into undercover reporter mode to get the lowdown on Mr Trump's visit.

"What was it like having Mr Trump to dinner?" I asked, casually.

"I don't know, it was my day off," came the reply, accompanied by trumpet blasts from beneath the table nearby.

"But he posed for a picture with the staff."

Drat! My hopes of a world exclusive were already in a bunker.

Not to worry, we would follow in his culinary footsteps for the night. So in went an order for foie gras for my wife, exactly what Mr Trump had reportedly ordered, while I opted for scallops.

The number of guests' cars outside was a sign of not only how popular the **Cock and Bull** was on a Saturday night, but also a possible warning that the service might be slow.

But not at all – our starters arrived in surprisingly quick time and that tempo was maintained throughout our stay.

Both were nicely presented on

the plate, just asking to be admired for a while before they were devoured. The first course was a story of contrasts.

The seared foie gras came with slices of crostini bread and an accompanying red onion and marmalade sauce.

My pan-fried scallops were also floating in a sea of contrasts, with sweet and sour cherry tomatoes and ginger salad for company.

Both were a great introduction to our dinner, with the distinctive taste combinations bringing out the best in each other.

The waiting staff were quick and efficient, while alert to the needs of each table. That was good. In so many other establishments, the staff hardly look at the customers.

Following Mr Trump's example, I ordered an 8oz sirloin steak with tomato and mushroom, and I added a side order of mashed potato with cheese and chives.

My wife went for a fillet of beef and roast carrot and garlic purèe with a shallot and mushroom juice. A portion of hand-cut, home-made chips was also taken as a side order.

The steak was excellent in texture and consistency, but might have been a tad more cooked than the medium rare I ordered. The speciality mashed potato was a delicious, fluffy delight.

My wife's generous portion of beef, cooked medium rare, had a wonderful, deep red blush to it and just melted in her mouth. The rich juice and purèe complemented it perfectly. I helped her out with the excellent hand-cut chips, I have to confess.

Two exquisite puddings rounded things off in style. My wife went for a dark chocolate and Grand Marnier soufflé with orange créme anglaise and kumquat chutney (the menu advises that you allow fifteen minutes for this order).

Not to be outdone, I ordered white chocolate cheesecake with Baileys and a duo of strawberry, one served as ice cream and the other as berries in juice.

Our investigations into Mr Trump's eating habits had not finished. I could not resist the seductive charms of the marvellous home-made fudge he had tried, which came with our coffee.

The trail was now getting cold as we did not know what Mr Trump did next. Perhaps the editor will let us fly to New York to find out . . .

Quality of Food	5
Menu Choice	4
Surroundings	5
Location	4
Service	5
Value for Money	4
Total [out of 30]	**27**

L'Auberge at the County Hotel

32 High Street, Banff

telephone: 01261 815353   website: <u>www.thecountyhotel.com</u>

"County cuisine est formidable"

To experience a truly gastronomic sensation it is often said that you have to head to France.

In the north-east's case, Banff will do just as nicely. Mais oui, Banff!

The County Hotel, in the historic town's High Street, has been under the French influence since 1999, when Eric Pantel and his wife, Vida, a senior stewardess with British Airways, took it over.

Meals here are to die for – and we were not disappointed with our evening there under the watchful gaze of former prime minister Winston Churchill, just one of the many pictures that adorn the dining-room walls.

Winston's not the only statesman to grace the County; new Scottish First Minister Alex Salmond is a regular diner.

He was there the other Saturday for lunch ahead of the opening, at Banff's magnificent Duff House, of a new exhibition of paintings of scenes from Lossiemouth to Fraserburgh by John Lowrie Morrison – better known as Jolomo.

Our excursion to Banff could not have been better; it was one of those rare evenings in June when the sun made an appearance, brightening up the countryside and making the journey along the banks of the River Deveron from the depths of rural Aberdeenshire to its mouth between Banff and Macduff – most definitely in Banffshire – all the more pleasing.

The welcome from Mrs Pantel was warm and we were shown downstairs to the bistro for pre-dinner drinks and to make our selections.

There's not one, but three menus at the County, and all wonderfully Gallic – the simpler menu, l'Auberge; the more sophisticated menu, gourmand, and then the à la carte which, given Banff's location, has an appealing seafood selection.

All the menus had dishes to tantalise, but after discussion we selected items from the menu gourmand. That said, we could have mixed and matched between each of the menus.

For starters, it was salads all round – warm monkfish for the fisherman, smoked salmon for me and the champêtre pâté for she who must be obeyed.

It's not often that I can compliment a salad, but the County's is exquisite. The dressing tingled taste buds that had not been stimulated for years, while the tomatoes actually tasted like tomatoes as opposed to the insipid offerings that supermarkets regularly pass off these days as 'quality'. The pâté was sensational, and there was an interesting twist as a passion fruit was served with my smoked salmon.

Mains were equally good. My sirloin steak, served with a flambée sauce, was melt in the mouth. There was exactly the same comment about the duck confit, while the poached salmon – very tasty – went down a treat.

The fisherman does not often comment on presentation, but he was amazed by the artistic talents, especially the way in which the potatoes were displayed around the plate.

Would we have dessert? Well, with a selection that included crème brulée, tiramisu, lemon panna cotta, tarte tatin, sticky toffee pudding, chocolat marbre, bread and butter pudding, tarte aux citrons and meringue nests, there wasn't really any response other than yes for the other two. I went for biscuits and cheese.

Our chef came to inquire twice during our meal if we were enjoying it. Of that there was absolutely no doubt, although as an Aberdonian, I have to tackle him on his assertion that beef from France's Charolais cattle breed is the best.

Our favoured wine was not in stock, but on the recommendation of Mrs Pantel we went with the French Gigondas 2004. Lighter definitely, but just as good and a perfect partner for a wonderful evening that finished watching the sun setting over Macduff through the dining-room windows.

Quality of Food	5
Menu Choice	5
Surroundings	4
Location	4
Service	5
Value for Money	5
Total *[out of 30]*	**28**

The Green Inn
9 Victoria Road, Ballater

telephone: 01339 755701   website: www.green-inn.com

"A mouth-watering journey of discovery"

A good chef feeds you well; a great chef takes your tastebuds on a journey – and it's a place you want to go.

After our visit to the **Green Inn**, Ballater, I just hope the chef isn't planning on hitting the road anytime soon.

When I called the "restaurant with rooms" to book, I could tell this was going to be worth the trip when I was asked if a vegetarian menu would be required. The choice of main courses that night would be duck, halibut, Scottish lamb or Aberdeen Angus beef,

I was told, so I appreciated the heads-up, being a bit veggie.

When we arrived, we were warmly welcomed into a comfortable sitting-room by a smiling host. This is Trevor, who makes himself useful at front of house while his wife Evelyn and son Chris work their magic behind kitchen doors..

We sat back on plump sofas and admired the elegant interiors while surveying the inventive menu, obviously designed with quality in mind, not quantity.

How does "seared breast of Gressingham duck with wild rice and roasted figs, confit leg, foie gras and cep lasagna in thyme jus" sound?

Over aperitifs we made our choices, and then were led through to a warmly decorated conservatory, from where you could admire a pretty courtyard garden. Tables were spaced generously so that conversations could be intimate, and Trevor and his friendly assistant made us feel right at home.

Attention to detail was impressive, from the menu to the ambience to the choice of freshly baked walnut or saffron bread rolls.

Starters were a choice of ravioli of Loch Fyne scallops, warm salad of peppered roe deer, grilled fillet of sea bass and slow-braised Perthshire wild boar, with the vegetarian option being a warm salad of chargrilled vegetables.

However, as the dessert menu was making our mouths water, we opted for an appetiser and two courses.

For a main course, my husband chose the seared fillet of Aberdeen Angus beef with pan-fried foie gras, smoked pomme purée, caramelised baby onions and wild mushrooms in a red wine reduction.

He said the pink-centred beef was the best and most tender he had had. A sword of "delicious" creamy mashed potato was drawn across the plate and he was impressed by the immaculate presentation.

Mine was to be wild mushroom lasagna with roasted garlic, baby vegetables and thyme velouté. Although this was the only vegetarian main course, it turned out to be magnificent. Looking like a labour of love, it was topped with a stack of delicately shredded crispy onions, and every mouthful was a surprise.

The difference between good and great food is down to the ingenuity of the chef and his ability to mix and blend taste sensations. And this was the nicest blend of flavours, textures and ingredients we've both experienced for quite some time.

The signs had been good from the arrival of the appetisers – small cups of cappuccino of parsnip with curry oil – which was soup that looked like mousse that tasted wonderful.

The tantalising journey came close to an end with our desserts of choice. A warm chocolate fondant cookie with a delicate cinnamon stick parfait and rich chocolate sauce, and a raspberry soufflé with mascarpone sorbet. Both arrived to the "wows" of the American group seated nearby, and our ensuing "mmmms" and "oohs" obviously helped them with their own choices.

And finally, the coffee and petit fours arrived with the cutest chocolate-encrusted passion fruit sorbet ice lollies, designed of course to cleanse the palate. And they did.

Our coffee was topped up as required – a refreshing touch – and if we could have moved in there permanently, my bags were packed already.

I would defy any bon viveur worth his salt to find fault with the food here. This was, quite frankly, as close to perfection as it gets. Had the restaurant been located not five yards from my own front door, it would have scored full marks.

Quality of Food	5
Menu Choice	5
Surroundings	5
Location	4
Service	5
Value for Money	5
Total [out of 30]	**29**

The Inn at Heath Hill

Muir Road, Memsie, Fraserburgh

telephone: 01346 541492   website: www.theinnatheathhill.com

"Country cooking at its best"

A restaurant in the north of Buchan is ensuring that the area's reputation for hospitality is kept alive and well – without breaking the bank.

We visited **The Inn at Heath Hill**, at Memsie, near Fraserburgh, for Sunday lunch and left suitably impressed.

Value for money abounds. The most expensive starter was just £5.95, while the top-priced main course – a braised lamb shank – was £11.50.

Steaks are obviously more expensive, but at £17.95 for a sirloin and £21.95 for a fillet, they, too, are well priced to give many other restaurants a run for their money.

Our three-course lunch for three with drinks and coffee at just a tad over £79 was excellent.

Mother – she who must be obeyed – had been suitably impressed after calling to book. She said it was by far the most pleasant booking experience she had encountered.

Our welcome at the inn – on the road between Memsie and Ardlaw Farm – was warm and we were given a choice of eating either in the bar area or conservatory. We chose the latter, although it was a little chilly given the howling gale outside.

The antique irons that adorn the conservatory windowsills provoked an interesting pre-lunch discussion as we mulled over the menu. Let's just say that, in our household, there is only one person suitably qualified to use an iron.

That person is not male and she was of the view that it was high time someone else learned the craft. My father and I were, however, of a different opinion. It was perhaps just as well the waitress appeared to take the lunch order so that the conversation could be steered in a different direction.

For me, it was the Iceland prawns bound in Marie-Rose sauce, served with salad leaves and brown bread. Mother had the chicken liver pate with oatcakes and tomato chutney, while father, as ever, opted for the soup of the day, lentil and cumin.

We were all happy with our choices, although the salad leaves that accompanied the prawns became an unnecessary addition with the sirloin steak I ordered as a main. The steak was cooked to perfection, medium rare, but I would have much preferred vegetables with it.

Mother's main was the special of roast beef with Yorkshire pudding, roast potatoes, parsnips and turnip. She asked for just one slice of beef, but ended up with several in what was a rather large portion.

Strangely, father decided on fish.

He was, however, more than happy with the fillet of plaice baked with prawns and double cream, topped with parsley sauce and served with vegetables and potatoes.

Other mains on the menu included what you would expect in a country pub – beef-steak burger, duck breast, chicken curry, scampi, beef-steak lasagne and steak and ale casserole.

Despite the exceptionally large main courses, we all had desserts – two home-made rice puddings and an ice cream. The rice came with a portion of jam which may well have piled on the calories, but we were not really caring.

When we arrived at 12.30pm, we were the only folk there. By the time we left, though, both the conservatory and bar area were busy.

The service from such a young staff was very good. The food was without the complications of added jus and all sorts of other unnecessary adornments.

What we were served up was wholesome, good and simple.

The only mild criticism was that, while the beef and steaks proudly boasted on the menu that they came from Aberdeenshire and Mathers of Inverurie, there was no such geographical indicator for the lamb or the fish.

Buchan is home to two of Britain's biggest fishing ports – Peterhead for whitefish and

Fraserburgh for prawns. Strange then that the prawns for my starter were branded Iceland on a menu that says, "The Inn uses as many fresh ingredients and as much local produce as possible".

If using local produce, it is a good idea for restaurants to actually show it.

Other than that, **The Inn at** **Heath Hill** was country cooking and country hospitality at its best.

Quality of Food	5
Menu Choice	3
Surroundings	4
Location	4
Service	4
Value for Money	5
Total *[out of 30]*	**25**

Linsmohr Hotel

Oldmeldrum Road, Pitmedden, Aberdeenshire

telephone: 01651 842214   website: www.linsmohrhotel.co.uk

"Coming up roses"

I was somewhat perturbed as owner/chef Drew Leil burst out of his kitchen and strode towards me, although he did look quite resplendent in his black and white striped trousers, I have to say.

Drew smiled and thanked us warmly for travelling from Aberdeen to sample his culinary skills, but that did nothing to ease my nerves.

I was wondering anxiously whether he knew that my wife and I were quaffing his wine. I don't mean the usual selections from his wine list, but something from his own personal stock – a sixteen-year-old French bottle, and very nice, too.

His daughter, Rebecca, who looks after diners at the front of house, had pulled out all the stops to find a bottle of rosé from somewhere and, rather than let us down, she raided her dad's personal collection.

We really appreciated the gesture, but would Drew, more to the point? Of course it was OK with Drew – he had told Rebecca to search it out for us, it transpired.

We agreed that it was a lovely touch from our host.

As the night unfolded, this became the theme; they were warm and welcoming and nothing was too much trouble.

We had not realised what a treat we were in for at the **Linsmohr** as every dish turned out to be a delight.

It proved easy to find as we headed north out of Aberdeen and slipped off the A90 on to the B999 towards Pitmedden. The hotel stands in an attractive and solid granite building, set back from Oldmeldrum Road with ample parking space.

An entrance to the right takes you past the public bar, where there seemed to be much mirth and friendly high jinks going on, and into the lounge/restaurant.

The hall led us into a large, sprawling room that was almost the size of a dance hall or function room. Tucked into a corner was a small bar area and the dining tables and chairs lined the walls on a slightly raised area. Eye-catching stonework featured heavily, both around the walls and dividing the room at intervals.

Near the bar, a group of leather sofas stood around a wood-burning stove. This was a cosy place to relax, take a drink and study the menu.

The menu displayed a combination of set meals and specials, which are changed each Thursday. The selection was not huge, but it packed in a lot of variety and Drew and his wife, who are the creative force in the kitchen, were obviously playing to their strengths.

There was a strong emphasis on home-made specialities and top-quality produce from local suppliers.

For starters, I went for home-made haddock fish cakes while my wife homed in on deep-fried Camembert with cranberry sauce.

The Camembert was a great combination, with a crumbly outer coating giving way to the delicately

81

soft interior, both complemented by the contrasting fruitiness of the sauce.

The fish cakes were a delight, with a generous filling encased in a soft potato shell rather than batter or breadcrumbs.

The restaurant was quiet apart from two or three other couples with young children. It seemed a popular choice for family groups and the whole feel was very informal.

I mentioned it was quiet. That was not exactly accurate, judging by the whoops and merriment coming from the public bar and the giggles of the serving staff as they scurried between the two bars. The **Linsmohr** seemed the sort of place where everyone had a smile on their face, both staff and customers.

For mains, my wife went for an 8oz sirloin steak with home-made onion rings, tomatoes, mushrooms and mushroom sauce, with carrots, broccoli and chips.

My imagination had been captured by griddled Barbary duck, cut into slices, served on a bed of garlic mashed potato and drizzled with sweet chilli sauce.

The large, succulent steak was a real treat and as good as anything my wife had tasted elsewhere. I wish I'd had my camera with me so that I could have taken a picture of the home-made onion rings, which arrived towering above the steak.

They were the biggest I had ever seen. They looked like someone had thrown a set of quoits into the deep fryer.

My duck, cooked medium rare, arrived with the strips of meat arched up on to the small mountain of garlic mashed potatoes like small ladders. It was an eye-catching presentation and the taste contrasts were spot on.

From time to time, Rebecca would pass by to ask how we were doing. She would also linger to answer any questions we had about the dishes – or anything at all, for that matter.

When we got our second breath, we went for the puddings – and what a treat they were.

Belgian waffles, maple syrup and ice cream for my wife and the best cheesecake I had ever tasted for me – mallow and butterscotch, with ice cream.

We sat down in the comfy leather chairs by the fire again for a last drink and almost nodded off, so relaxed were we.

I thought it was good value for one of our best nights out in recent times.

It's a family affair at the **Linsmohr**, which is why they probably make so much effort to please.

As we left, a Highland jig was playing in the public bar, accompanied by the laughing voices we had heard earlier. I just knew what I would see when I glanced back, and I was not disappointed.

Sure enough, one of the locals was doing a jig, of sorts, with the aid of a bar stool as a partner. Yes, the **Linsmohr** is a happy place, we agreed.

Quality of Food	5
Menu Choice	4
Surroundings	3
Location	4
Service	5
Value for Money	5
Total *[out of 30]*	**26**

Moonlight Tandoori

34 Balmellie Street, Turriff

telephone: 01888 562636

"Turriff tandoori in Westminster top ten"

It could never be said that Turriff, in the heart of Aberdeenshire, was ever on the culinary map.

The town's Indian restaurant is, however, attempting to change that and has, in recent weeks, achieved national recognition.

The **Moonlight Tandoori** got through to the final ten in the annual Tiffin Cup, entrants for which are nominated by Britain's MPs.

It was Alex Salmond, the Banff and Buchan MP and Scottish First Minister, who put forward the eatery that is housed in what used to be the restaurant of the local mart before it was shut in the late-1980s.

Moonlight Tandoori qualified for final cook-offs in the House of Commons but unfortunately for it – and Turriff – it did not win the overall award.

Still, to come in the final ten from sixty-six of the country's best Indian restaurants is no mean feat and one of which the staff are obviously extremely proud, judging by the pictures they have of Mr Salmond, as well as Cabinet Office Minister Ed Miliband and celebrity chef Ainsley Harriott, adorning the walls.

I have to own up immediately and say that I am something of a virgin when it comes to Indian food. I can count on the fingers of both hands how many occasions I have visited such eateries.

I therefore took cold feet at the thought of trying the chicken balti lahore, the signature dish of chef Mohammed Belal which got the **Moonlight Tandoori** through to the Tiffin Cup final.

It did look tempting, especially as it is prepared with what the menu says is a special balti sauce that consists of twenty different herbs and spices. Those herbs, it has to be said, were very fresh as

they were being delivered as I sat at my table in the corner poring over the menu.

But baltis, I fear, are just too hot for me, so I stuck with one of the chef's other, milder recommendations. Mr Salmond would appear to have a stronger constitution than I.

The restaurant has a very light and contemporary feel. Blue and white are the order of the day.

The waiting staff were very pleasant and full of smiles. The restaurant was also very busy for a Monday evening, although in a town where there are precious few places to eat out that is perhaps not surprising. Other diners included former Grampian TV newsreader John Duncanson, who disappeared off the small screen many years ago.

My meal started off with poppadoms complete with onions and mango chutney. This was followed by the starters – chicken and prawn spicy rolls, and akin to the spring rolls served in Chinese restaurants.

Moonlight Tandoori offers a huge choice of mains, including masala, passanda, Madras, vindaloo, dupiaza, rogan josh, korai, jalfrezie, kurma, malaya and dansak dishes, to name but a few.

I, however, opted for one of the chef's special recommendations – roshni lamb. September was, after all, Scotland's annual Festival of

Lamb, which is being promoted by Quality Meat Scotland.

The roshni was a wonderfully mild curry and allowed the delicate flavours to flow from it. It was cooked with a range of spices, coriander and green chilli, as well as cloves of garlic.

Delicious it proved to be, and it was complemented beautifully by the house special pilau rice I ordered to go with it.

To soak up the sauce, I had a keema naan. I've had naan bread before but this one came with the addition of a spicy mincemeat. Very tasty.

Coffee rounded off my dinner just as the restaurant got busier.

I have to say that I was very impressed with the dining experience.

My only complaint, and a minor one at that, was that the smiling staff should perhaps be a little more attentive as other diners did not have menus taken away after they ordered their meals and one customer who ordered a red wine got it long after her dining companions.

Quality of Food	5
Menu Choice	5
Surroundings	4
Location	4
Service	4
Value for Money	4
Total [out of 30]	**26**

Castleton House Hotel and Restaurant

by Glamis, Angus

telephone: 01307 840340   website: <u>www.castletonglamis.co.uk</u>

"Just grand"

Eating out in a grand country house always brings a sense of occasion.

So when my mother and I decided to dine out, I had no hesitation in choosing **Castleton House Hotel**, near Glamis.

This 100-year-old house is hidden by tall trees, fostering a special, secluded atmosphere.

It has also been awarded two AA rosettes, grouping it among Scotland's elite restaurants, and it currently holds the highest grading awarded to any hotel in Angus.

So an excellent culinary pedigree, along with a beautiful setting,

should pretty much guarantee to come up with the goods.

Our visit was on the eve of the popular extravaganza held at the imposing Glamis Castle nearby, so the beautiful vintage cars sailing along the roads before us only added to my Merchant Ivory imaginings as we swept up the drive.

After admiring the awards and recognition which line the walls – along with an eclectic mix of art – we made our way to the cosy bar and settled into comfy club chairs.

There was a private sixtieth party on through the house which sounded loud and posh as we glimpsed the cocktail dresses and heard the chink of champagne glasses.

We were eating in the conservatory, which is bright with its red tiled floor and green painted tables.

The menu is compact, but with enough to tempt you. We both went for red meat, but there was grilled sea bass on the go, along with pan-fried guinea fowl. There was no choice for the vegetarian, which is unusual, but I imagine a kitchen this accomplished would rustle something up.

Slender slices of baked salmon appeared before our meal as we idly chatted, tempting our taste buds for what was to come.

I had the carpaccio of North Sea halibut to start, which was beautifully presented on a bed of roquette salad with salsa verde sauce, topped with west-coast crab which resembled seafood coleslaw and tasted marvellous.

Mother went for a chicken Caesar salad, which she said was perfectly serviceable – crispy lettuce, creamy dressing, anchovies and Parmesan, all present and correct and served in an ideal starter portion size.

She said this shortly before tucking into her medallions of beef, which she had chosen for main course, again nicely presented, with dauphinoise potatoes, baby spinach and red wine shallots. She judged the beef a little overcooked, but seemed quite satisfied with the overall dish.

Meanwhile, I was marvelling at my venison. OK, I was having hunting, shooting and fishing fantasies, but brought myself back to earth to enjoy fully the amazing red onion marmalade and beetroot jus, which were perfect with roast venison, I have to say. A bit of curly kale and I was in heaven.

The waitresses were very pleasant and helpful, and what they lacked in experience they certainly made up for in enthusiasm, with just the right amount of concern for our welfare.

I did wonder who made them wear such a strange shade of blue as it made them all slightly resemble Tesco workers, but that's the old-fashioned streak in me. Waiting staff should be in black and white. Or maybe I'm just behind the times and Tesco is the way forward.

I bowed out of sweets to sample the Ian Mellis cheeseboard, which was a very good choice, with smoked cheese, soft cheese, hard cheese and goat's cheese all lined up for my delectation with warmed, yes warmed, oatcakes on the side and a little chutney for good measure.

However, mother caved in to a pear tarte tatin with honeycomb ice cream and butterscotch sauce, which was tooth-achingly sweet, but a lovely end to the meal.

In all, it is dining for a special occasion, but with such a beautiful location and excellent food, I would thoroughly recommend a jaunt to Glamis.

Quality of Food	5
Menu Choice	4
Surroundings	5
Location	4
Service	4
Value for Money	4
Total *[out of 30]*	**26**

Kookaburras

Arbroath Road, by Forfar

telephone: 01307 818005   website: www.kookaburras.co.uk

"Far from the Outback"

So there I was, enjoying Sunday lunch with the family in a themed restaurant.

The scenario does sound a bit unlikely, I grant you, but believe me, it depends entirely on your choice of restaurant.

On this occasion, we were in one of Angus's best-kept secrets,

Kookaburras, enjoying its carvery.

I say best-kept secrets, but the place was going like a fair, so obviously I'm just one of the last to catch on.

The restaurant sits in a peaceful countryside setting just two miles from Forfar and I have been before to sample its formidable high tea.

However, my brother had been extolling the virtues of the carvery to me for weeks, so my mother, aunt and I met up with him and his charming girlfriend to see what all the fuss was about.

We weren't alone. There were grannies and grandads, mothers and daughters, brothers and sisters, all contentedly munching on the excellent fare on offer.

We sauntered through to the buffet and, on seeing the marvellous spread laid out before us, we gasped as one.

For starters, there was potted prawn marie rose, peppered mackerel, smoked salmon, pâté and oatcakes, green salads with and without dressings, and a steaming tureen of home-made soup.

This was before we got anywhere near the main courses. Here, there was stroganoff, chilli beef with nachos, guacamole, salsa and soured cream and a beef stew to negotiate before you got to your grinning host, Darren, who was presiding over the roast beef and pork.

These were all accompanied by gravy, apple sauce, roast potatoes and a selection of vegetables, as well as piping hot Yorkshire puddings.

There was even a choice of roast beef, depending on whether you preferred pink or medium.

All this without me even having glanced at the desserts and already

I was speechless. Many brotherly jokes followed about the possibility of me ever being speechless, but it is quite a sight to see.

But I should really get back to the theming element. Darren is from Down Under, and this is fairly evident from the surroundings. Should you have missed the life-sized kangaroo carving and the eerily lifelike Steve Irwin sculpture on the way in, then the Aboriginal art and the framed Shane Warne shirt on the walls provide another valuable clue.

And this is without mentioning the wallabies, rheas and emus which quietly graze in the nearby enclosures while parrots swing from one side of their outdoor cage to another. The antipodean influence is hard to miss.

But all this makes it a very family-friendly location with patient staff and plenty for the family to see and do.

Meanwhile, my family had seen and done quite a lot, having polished off enough food to fuel a trek across the Outback, but undeterred, we made the final foray, this time to the dessert selection.

And what a selection. There was mango pavlova, lemon gateau, vanilla cheesecake and beautiful fresh fruit salad, as well as the gooiest sticky toffee pudding you ever beheld. But the crowning touch was definitely the chocolate fondue merrily cascading its cocoa waterfall shaded by long skewers of marshmallows.

So, as we sat back, exchanging family news and mulling over the latest Forfar gossip, I reflected on the entirely successful choice of venue – laid-back, friendly and with delicious food.

Strewth, I might even get

together with the rellies a bit more often.

Quality of Food	4
Menu Choice	5
Surroundings	4
Location	4
Service	4
Value for Money	5
Total [out of 30]	**26**

Lochside Lodge and Roundhouse Restaurant
Bridgend of Lintrathen, near Kirriemuir

telephone: 01575 560340   website: www.lochsidelodge.com

"Late lunch"

It was one of those days when the chances of dining out for lunch were diminishing by the minute.

We'd heard of a place called The **Lochside Lodge and Roundhouse Restaurant**, near

Kirriemuir, Angus, that had earned a good reputation for its quality food prepared by joint proprietor and award-winning chef Graham Riley, a Master Chef of Great Britain.

So it was with watering mouths

and rumbling stomachs that we set off on our journey south to experience the fine food we'd heard so much about. We were aiming to get there for lunch at 1.30pm – last orders being at 1.45pm. All seemed to be going well until a series of hold-ups on the A90 meant we were getting dangerously close to missing out on lunch altogether.

We actually arrived just after 1.45pm and the restaurant was empty. Things were not looking good. But – perhaps feeling sorry for us – chef agreed to keep the kitchen open just for us.

We were shown to our table inside the converted steading – a bright, relaxed area with old church pews for seating and large windows converted from barn doors. Adding to the rustic feel of the place was a large collection of sporting and farming memorabilia, all displayed on the wood-panelled ceiling and original stone walls.

All lunches are served in the steading, which has a more informal atmosphere than the **Roundhouse Restaurant**, where evening meals are served.

Although impressed by our surroundings, being the only two diners meant that we could hear a pin drop, and the atmosphere was a little tense. However, service was quick!

Drinks and menus were before us in no time at all and we promptly perused the menu to see what would impress our taste buds the most.

There was a good choice of starters and main courses on offer, but it was the terrine of chicken and vegetables wrapped in sweet-cured bacon with a redcurrant dressing that took my fancy, while the thinly sliced smoked duck with toffee roasted peanuts appealed more to my husband's taste.

Our orders were placed and it was now a case of waiting to see whether we would get a rushed version of the dishes because chef was waiting to clock off.

After about ten minutes, the food arrived and I have to say that the presentation was excellent. No corners had been cut and it was obvious that the food had been prepared by someone who takes pride in his work.

Large white plates provided the perfect backdrop to an array of colours provided by the neat, delicately stacked food before us. It certainly looked good – almost too good to eat.

Each dish was bursting with flavour, with the combination of fresh herbs, dressing and the natural flavours of the chicken and vegetables all exciting the taste buds with every mouthful.

The smoked duck melted in the mouth and the toffee roasted peanuts were described as "fantastic".

For a main course, I opted for

91

the char sui Perthshire pork with jasmine rice and chilli dressing while my husband went for the Aberdeen-Angus beef steak with reduced redcurrant jus and mash potato.

Again, service was unsurprisingly quick, but as with the starters, presentation was impressive.

My pork dish was rich in Oriental flavour and included just about the right combination of meat and vegetables in a stir-fry fashion. I'm often concerned that the presence of chilli in these dishes can overpower the flavour, but in this case, it was not too strong and simply added a slight kick to the dish.

The beef steak was cooked perfectly for my husband and was both tender and tasty. He did comment that, although his meal was enjoyable, there was nothing that made it particularly outstanding, unlike the starter he had just enjoyed.

Although conscious of the time, the proprietors seemed perfectly happy to offer us desserts. I had a very simple strawberry meringue with cream and my husband chose a layered tiramisu.

The meringue was topped with fresh strawberries, which were delicious, but there was nothing that made the dessert particularly moreish. The tiramisu, on the other hand, was praised for its rich taste and was nicely soaked in liqueur.

From a journey that had started so badly, we were expecting the worst for our dining experience. But we were impressed that the chef went to so much trouble to prepare good-quality food that definitely put the day back on the right track.

Quality of Food	4
Menu Choice	4
Surroundings	4
Location	4
Service	5
Value for Money	5
Total [out of 30]	**26**

Sultan Turkish Restaurant

127 Castle Street, Forfar

telephone 01307 467941

"Turkish delight"

There are many things I like about Forfar. Queuing outside McLarens the baker on a Saturday lunchtime for a bridie, strolling around the loch and poking about in pretty gift shops are but a few of my favourite things.

A highlight of any visit, though, is always the **Sultan Turkish Restaurant** on Castle Street.

It always struck me as strange that you could find such a good place for Turkish food in a relatively small Angus town, but since it opened many years ago, it has upheld high standards and has become something of an institution.

We rolled up of a weekend evening – booking is always recommended, as it can get incredibly busy – and were shown to our seats by a charming waitress.

The **Sultan** has quite a minimal feel, with the basics being laid out on pristine white tables, but the contemporary Turkish music, the artefacts at the bar and the interesting art on the walls all combine to give the place an eclectic and laid-back feel.

The open kitchen is just by the door so you can watch your meal being prepared, should you wish, or just sit back and enjoy the wafting smells of cooking with a glass of Turkish wine.

Starters are quite varied, from hummus and halloumi to dolma – vine leaves filled with rice, onions and pine kernels – and cacik, which is chopped spinach in a creamy garlic yoghurt.

I chose the kizartma, which was slender slices of aubergine smeared with yoghurt and a delicately spiced tomato sauce.

It appeared as a perfect starter portion and tickled my taste buds just enough to prepare me for the main event.

My dining partner chose the sucuk, which is a spicy beef sausage, drawn as he is to anything involving red meat.

This had been recommended to him by my brother, as everyone in Forfar is an expert on Turkish cuisine, and it proved to be a top tip for the carnivore.

Our appetites suitably whetted, we sat back waiting for our main courses.

All the dishes are served with pitta bread and salad, drenched in a superb Mediterranean dressing. There are a couple of choices for the vegetarian, but in the main, it is meat-eaters who can feast their eyes and appetites.

Spit-roasted lamb, specially marinaded chicken, sis köfte, skewered portions of minced lamb and the döner so beloved by the

Scottish people are all on offer. You can have a dish of one, a dish of two, or even a selection of them all.

Some are served on a bed of rice, some on a bed of pitta bread, some with yoghurt, and nearly all with the spicy tomato sauce that pops up throughout the menu.

I went for the Iskender kebab because I like the yoghurt mixed in with my tomato sauce and the plump rice, and also you get a selection of meat so you don't feel like you've missed out on anything and there's no dish envy at what's across the table.

It was as good as ever, the meat deliciously cooked and the presentation immaculate.

I might still have felt slight envy at the **Sultan** special opposite me as skewered minced lamb, chicken and vegetables were put down in a mighty great portion.

For dessert, my companion went for classic baklava, which was beautifully prepared, oozing honey with ice cream melting over the top.

However, I always have to have the pineapple delight, a confection designed to appeal to the inner child in anyone, with marshmallows, crushed pineapple and whipped cream.

I like to think it is an exotic concoction from the back streets of Istanbul. Alas, apparently it is more WRI church hall than Hagia Sophia, but this will not stop me ordering it on my next, and possibly every subsequent, visit. Pure unadulterated pleasure in every spoonful.

We thoroughly enjoyed our meal and, for three courses and a bottle of extremely drinkable Turkish wine, it was reasonably priced.

The waitress was chatty and friendly and nothing was too much bother for her. The kitchen staff are as involved as front of house, being so on display, and they were equally pleasant and helpful.

With the amount of regular custom, there is general banter, but everyone is welcomed with a warm smile.

I have eaten many a meal over the years at the **Sultan**, all of a consistently high standard, but my companion was a Turkish novice so I could check that my judgment wasn't being clouded.

Rest assured, dear readers, the verdict was unanimous. The **Sultan** does indeed still reign supreme.

Quality of Food	5
Menu Choice	4
Surroundings	4
Location	4
Service	5
Value for Money	4
Total [out of 30]	**26**

Coast

104 George Street, Oban

telephone: 01631 569900   website: www.coastoban.com

"An Oban treasure"

It was one of those days when everything that could go wrong did just that.

The noon arrival in Oban was delayed by an hour thanks to unannounced roadworks on the A85 between Tyndrum and Dalmally.

I suppose we should be thankful that the Scottish Executive has, after several years, finally got to grips with the potholes that have dogged the road at Glen Lochy. Then again, there's simply no excuse for not having up signs warning of roadworks ahead, in much the same way that the bridge replacement work at Glencoe was announced at Tyndrum.

Now that I've got that off my chest, I can also tell you that the evening meeting I had to attend started an hour late and finished just before 8pm.

That meant a quick dash back to the hotel before meeting friends for drinks.

At 8.30pm, many eateries in other towns across Scotland would be shut. Thankfully, in Oban, they remain open.

We had intended returning to the wonderful Ee-Usk on the pier, but as we walked along George Street, the very trendy **Coast** shone out like a beacon, with candles in its windows.

Sandwiched between two of Oban's fish-and-chip shops, this restaurant, run by Richard and Nicola Fowler, is housed in a former bank.

To **Coast's** credit, you can find out all that it serves on the menu by the door.

Our taste buds suitably tantalised, we entered and found an elegantly designed eatery where the staff were particularly pleasant. They apologised countless times for our table beside the radiator, but what they didn't know was that we had been exposed to the elements for an afternoon and the heat was particularly welcome.

The three of us had each decided on something different to test the chef, and none of us was disappointed.

My whole grilled Loch Linnhe langoustines with salad leaves, garlic and parsley butter were outstanding. This doubles as both a starter and a main course.

The real treat was in the choice of the young lady. Her hot and cold smoked salmon was unquestionably a rare find. Presentation here was superb, with the cold salmon served as a pâté in a small pot along with thinly sliced smoked salmon. I could have sworn the cold salmon was from the Loch Awe Smokehouse, but will no doubt hear if I'm wrong.

My other dining companion had the west coast crab salad, a delightful combination of crab with

Parmesan tuile, tomato and sweet pepper dressing.

Coast excelled in the main courses, too. I chose the fillet of Scottish pork wrapped in Parma ham with a Stornoway black pudding and date stuffing, Arran mustard mash and wild mushroom and red wine.

The pork was cooked a treat and well complemented by the pudding from the world's best purveyor of black pudding, Charlie 'Barley' MacLeod. The Arran mustard mash was the perfect combination, with the mustard adding that extra zing to the tatties.

The kitchen delivered an excellent pan-fried monkfish served with green beans, spiced cauliflower, potatoes and a vermouth sauce. The monkfish was done to perfection, delightfully moist. There was also an artist at work as the cauliflower was not served in chunks as is normal, but cut into tiny florets.

The sirloin steak was full of flavour and done, just as asked, at medium rare. Not a chip in sight, either.

We shouldn't really have had desserts, but did. I had the cheese (Dunsyre Blue and Isle of Mull) and biscuits, while the others had a rhubarb tart with home-made ginger ice cream and the chocolate and pistachio mousse with home-made cherry ice cream.

There was a trio of voices saying well done with the ginger ice cream. Wow would be the only word that does it justice.

We washed dinner down with a bottle of Baron de Le Stac Reserve, a 2002 Medoc – wonderfully crisp and fruity.

Coast is, like Ee-Usk, a treasure for Oban, especially when the town these days seems to be filled with bus-tour parties who are not exactly noted for fine dining.

Coast acts the part, with a menu to cater for every taste, excellent service and some real starch in the napkins.

Quality of Food	5
Menu Choice	4
Surroundings	4
Location	4
Service	5
Value for Money	5
Total *[out of 30]*	**27**

Knipoch House Hotel

Knipoch (six miles south of Oban on the A816 to Lochgilphead)

telephone: 01852 316251   website: www.knipochhotel.co.uk

"Knipoch a real discovery"

It had been one of those delightful days in Argyll when the sun shone and the rain stayed away.

We'd lunched wonderfully well on half a lobster and a pint of proper beer at the Tigh-an-Truish Hotel at Clachan, just beside the Bridge over the Atlantic, which you cross to get to the island of Seil.

A meeting of like-minded souls and the addition of a few others made for the perfect lunch before we set about exploring Seil and one of its neighbouring islands.

The big question as we took the little car ferry across to Luing was where dinner would be. Would we head back to Oban, return to the little pub where we had such a

delicious lunch or go somewhere we had not tried before?

Well, this was a journey of discovery so we opted for the latter, which was, in hindsight, the best option of them all, as we found a real treat.

Knipoch House Hotel is just a matter of yards from the Seil Island junction on the A816 that winds its way south of Oban to Lochgilphead.

With its yellow walls, **Knipoch** was just the welcoming beacon we needed as the sun began its descent in the west and the midges started to appear.

The home of the Craig family and a four-star hotel owned by them since 1981, **Knipoch** comes with a history, as Campbell, Thane of Cawdor, was assassinated here in 1592.

There were going to be no assassinations this evening; just three weary souls who would devour their dinner with gusto after an afternoon spent in Scotland's great outdoors.

Large gins ordered, we settled in the lounge with the menus and took in the gorgeous view. The bar, with its many, varied single malts, wasn't a match for the Pot Still, the Glasgow hostelry for whisky lovers, and which is financially supported by three of us regularly.

Knipoch's selection would do for the evening, although we opted for the Isle of Skye blend latterly which was considerably more than a decent Highland Park at our beloved whisky paradise in the Mean City's Hope Street.

The **Knipoch's** menu made you salivate. There was not much on it, but what there was made you sit up and take note.

Two of us chose the smoked salmon, while the third opted for the mussels.

The smoked salmon was in a word – wow! From Loch Creran, this salmon is cured, then marinated in juniper, rowan, Barbados sugar, herbs and whisky, and then smoked over oak for three days. The whole process is done at the hotel. The taste is absolutely out of this world. If it were packaged and sold, I would have bought a box of it and taken it home.

The Loch Etive mussels, served in a wonderfully creamy and tasty shallot, garlic and Chardonnay sauce, were a taste sensation, too.

But while the main courses were good, there was just a little niggle with them.

Two of us went for the Chateau Briand, a most unusual item these days on any menu. At **Knipoch**, the Aberdeen-Angus beef is served with a Béarnaise sauce (made from egg yolk, onion, tarragon and fresh herbs), Savoy cabbage, carrots, fried potatoes and green beans.

The beef was wonderful, but the vegetables just a trifle overdone and the potatoes a little soggy for my liking.

The other main was the Gressingham roast duck with a Bordelaise sauce made from stock reduced with onions, mushroom, red wine and thyme.

I've yet to be impressed by duck and I'm afraid this one proved a little chewy for my dining companion who, judging by the conversation, is counting the days down to retirement.

Our mains were accompanied by a deliciously fruity Campo Viego Reserva 1999 Rioja. It is another that will have to be added to the ever-lengthening list of riojas that I like.

The two sweet-toothed ones opted for dessert. I went for the biscuits and Scottish cheese, which came in the form of Dunsyre Blue, Mull of Kintyre and caboc.

The rich, dark chocolate terrine served with home-made ice cream and a raspberry coulis sauce looked a calorie counter's nightmare, but disappeared speedily from the plate.

He who ordered the liqueur ice cream initially had concerns that he couldn't taste the Drambuie, but then he hadn't noticed the ice cream was floating on top of a very large measure of Bonnie Prince Charlie's special elixir. Age is, quite obviously, getting the better of him.

The meal ended, we retired to the bar for an evening of conviviality over drams and some amazingly good Kenyan coffee made from beans freshly roasted on the premises.

It was expensive, but then the food was good, albeit with some very minor disappointments.

Quality of Food	4
Menu Choice	5
Surroundings	5
Location	4
Service	5
Value for Money	4
Total [out of 30]	**27**

Bon Appétit

22-26 Exchange Street, Dundee

telephone: 01382 809000   website: www.bonappetit-dundee.com

"Hitting the right spot, Bon Appétit"

Have you heard the one about the Dundonian who spent a sizeable chunk of his working life in France and then gave up his high-flying career in marketing to return home and open his own French restaurant?

Step forward John Batchelor and his wife, Audrey, owners of **Bon Appétit**, named in a local poll as the city's best place to dine in 2005.

It's a reverse of the situation one comes across all too frequently when holidaying in foreign climes – the English pub with a mine host scraping a living serving warm John Smiths and baked beans to those who cannot survive a fortnight without a generous helping of home comforts.

It's also a potential recipe for disaster, but the Batchelors have pulled off their gamble with some style.

Bon Appétit, tucked away down a quiet side street minutes from the city centre, has an authentic bistro feel to it, and while the walls adorned with pages from *Le Figaro* and a host of other French newspapers are somewhat stereotypical of the British view of a French eaterie, everything is Gallic.

Apart from the Shetland ice-cream, which we shall come back to later.

Our visit to the City of Discovery coincided with a visit to one of the increasingly popular continental markets. By the time of the appointed hour, we already had one foot in mainland Europe, having been tempted by the aroma of German sausage, French cheese and Belgian waffles.

We completed our virtual hop across the Channel when we were shown to a table which had, as its next-door neighbour, a party of four from, yes, France.

My schoolboy French makes me less than an expert, but I did manage to pick up on at least one "formidable", a couple of "très bien" and, if my hearing wasn't deceiving me, a "magnifique" was in there as well.

So the French people enjoyed their experience.

Our evening began with a warm welcome from Audrey, who made a return to her native city a year ahead of her husband to learn the restaurant business working in a local hotel.

She clearly packed a lot into her crash course, as the service could not be faulted throughout a pleasant evening.

We settled on a bottle of La Forge Chardonnay to accompany our meal and, the important part of the business out of the way, perused the menu to decide which food would accompany our wine.

I have a weakness for goat's cheese, so its pairing with raspberries in a tart was an obvious choice for me, while across the table the penchant for seafood surfaced as mussels were ordered, cooked from a choice of three varieties in white wine, garlic and shallots.

The tart was better than average, with the pastry deserving special mention. The mussels came complete with the obligatory French stick to mop up the tasty liquid. These were as good as any sampled on excursions to France and those at the adjacent table were très bien-ing at their main course portion of the same dish.

My braised beef in a garlic cream sauce, served with roasted pepper tagliatelle, had a melt in the mouth consistency and worked on every level.

The poussin poché-grillé au gingembre et citron vert was a fusion of Oriental flavour and French flair. Accompanied by a chilli and coconut rice with just the right amount of kick, it was served on a simple cucumber and yoghurt sauce. Perfect for a summer's evening.

From the choice of desserts, my eye was drawn to the true test of any French restaurant – crème brulée. I've had a few of these in the past, ranging from the passable to the edible, but **Bon Appétit's** effort was formidable.

Served in a wide, flat dish there was just enough crunch on top to marry with the moreish eggy custard underneath, infused liberally with vanilla seeds.

As we drained the last of the excellent wine, and examined a very respectable bill, we engaged John in conversation and it was clear that he and Audrey take a great deal of pride in the little corner of France they have transported to their home turf.

On this showing, they have

every right to be satisfied with their achievements.

And the Shetland ice cream? It's called Bloo Coo, and it went down a storm with the French. Perhaps an export opportunity?

Quality of Food	5
Menu Choice	5
Surroundings	4
Location	4
Service	5
Value for Money	4
Total *[out of 30]*	**27**

The Glass Pavilion
The Esplanade, Broughty Ferry, near Dundee

telephone: 01382 732738   website: www.theglasspavilion.co.uk

"A bright delight"

In the heady days of Scottish family seaside holidays, the beach pavilion at Broughty Ferry would have been packed with bathers attempting to thaw their extremities after a dip in the North Sea or plucking up the courage to brave the waters.

These days, the golden sands are all but deserted as people seek their annual dose of sun and sea in warmer climes.

Up and down the country, buildings such as the aforementioned pavilion have fallen into a state of disrepair, victims of budding graffiti artists and the vagaries of the Scottish weather.

But on the outskirts of Dundee, an architectural gem has been created on the esplanade with the addition of a bold and modern extension.

The Glass Pavilion is a beach-side tearoom by day and, at weekends, a bistro by night. The food is as innovative as the building, resulting in a dining experience which can be described only as unique.

Our visit one Friday evening came on a day when glorious summer sunshine had been replaced by dark, scudding clouds sweeping across the estuary of the River Tay.

The scene as we took our place at a window table – which, given

the nature of the building, could describe any of the seats in the house – was quite magnificent. The breeze was whipping the waves into foamy crests and someone not too far away was subject to a sizeable downpour.

By the time we had finished our excellent, if perhaps pricey, meal, the sky had turned a deep shade of blue, speckled with flecks of orange and red as the cloud gave way to a superb sunset.

The food? There was a reasonable choice across all three courses, covering most of the bases. Our selections were the breaded salmon and crab potato cake served with seasonal salad leaves and a chive butter sauce, and a pan-fried pave of wild mushroom and herb risotto, with Parmesan crisps and aged balsamic dressing.

Both dishes could have done with a little more seasoning, but this was a minor complaint.

The fish cake was sizeable and obviously freshly made, and worked well with the butter sauce.

The risotto had been moulded and pan-fried to give it a crispy coating, and while Parmesan crumbs would have been a more accurate description of one of its partners, they were tasty, as was the balsamic dressing.

The main courses were winners in every way. A fillet of Angus beef, served on a potato rösti with young vegetables and a Madeira jus, was succulent and rich, the dark sauce working perfectly with the meat, cooked medium as requested.

The pot au feu of corn-fed chicken breast, with a parsley potato purée and seasonal vegetables, was equally well received and, again, cooked to perfection.

Often, presentation is not matched by the eating experience, but I'm happy to report that **The Glass Pavilion** did not fall into the all show and no substance category.

One dessert was enough between two and the recommended glazed lemon and lime tart, while missing its promised fruit coulis, was a perfect blend of sweet and sour.

Coffee and a generous portion of tablet rounded things off nicely, as did the return of the sunshine.

The Glass Pavilion is not the easiest place to find, but take the trouble to seek it out and marvel at a piece of inspired architecture. Step inside and you won't be disappointed by the creations from the kitchen, either.

And if it's sunny, you could do worse than cross the road and go for a paddle.

Quality of Food	5
Menu Choice	4
Surroundings	5
Location	5
Service	4
Value for Money	4
Total [out of 30]	**27**

The Playwright

11 Tay Square, South Tay Street, Dundee

telephone: 01382 223113   website: www.theplaywright.co.uk

"A literary feast"

"If music be the food of love, play on". A famous literary line, but one which needs rewritten. What's that you say? Sacrilege? If you've had the pleasure of a visit to Dundee's newest fine-dining restaurant then you will understand where I'm coming from.

From now on it's "Who needs to play music, love the food".

OK, so it's not quite Shakespearean in its standards, but it does describe, literally, the quality of the entire experience at **The Playwright**.

We hadn't intended eating there, mainly due to the fact that we did

not know it existed. Our quest for somewhere to tempt the taste buds on Tayside was further hampered by this hidden gem being just that – hidden by scaffolding erected on the building which provides its home.

Fortunately, the owners had had the foresight to hang up a banner proclaiming its existence. This wasn't the most attractive piece of signage, but it did at least serve to bring the restaurant to our attention. Once we had tracked down the menu, we were hooked and simply had to have a table.

Except there were none. The staff couldn't have been more helpful, but friendly and welcoming is easy compared with making a table appear out of nowhere on a packed Saturday night. That is something more often reserved for Harry Potter and his Hogwarts chums.

As we prepared to troop off in search of somewhere else, which was always going to be second best, they pulled a rabbit from the hat. If we didn't mind dining early and being out by 7pm, they would fit us in.

That did the trick and, a couple of hours later, we were seated ready for the opening act of what turned out to be a memorable performance.

There was no children's menu, but that didn't put the younger members of the family off. They decided they could quite happily tackle the adult version of the pre-theatre table d'hôte.

But pre-theatre was a bit of a misnomer at **The Playwright**. The whole experience was a performance in itself, from the consistent quality of the service to the award-worthy efforts backstage.

The adults opted for starters – smoked haddock with baby spinach and a chive butter sauce, and cream of artichoke soup with parsley oil. The home-baked bread and butter, which appeared equally handcrafted, was a nice touch and kept the youngsters' hunger pangs at bay.

The fish was light and delicate, working perfectly with the sauce and the wilted greens. The soup was excellent, too, with a perfect texture and an interesting bite from the artichoke flavour.

For main course, both children opted for a medium sirloin of Scottish beef, one with the menu accompaniments of roast root vegetables, potato rösti and Bordelaise sauce, the other with some freshly cooked pasta.

The steaks were cooked as requested and the empty plates told their own story.

I opted for a supreme of pheasant with Savoy cabbage, fondant potatoes, black pudding and a thyme jus. The pheasant was good, if perhaps a little overcooked, and worked well with the black pudding.

My wife opted for the seared salmon with a confit of squid and sweet and sour sauce. The fish was, again, moist and delicate, and the slow-cooked squid a revelation. It was the dish over which there was most deliberation before the order was placed and yet turned out to be the clear winner in the taste stakes. Given the quality of everything else, that is praise indeed.

For dessert, we opted for one crème caramel with praline ice cream; one coconut tart with vanilla ice cream and marzipan syrup, and two terrine of chocolate served with mint chocolate syrup and white chocolate truffle.

Without wishing to be terribly

clichéd in theatrical terms, the final courses were worthy of a standing ovation. Each and every one was dessert heaven.

Much ado about nothing? Not a bit of it – this **Playwright** is a star in the making.

Quality of Food	4
Menu Choice	5
Surroundings	4
Location	5
Service	5
Value for Money	5
Total *[out of 30]*	**28**

Browns Bar and Brasserie

131–133 George Street, Edinburgh

telephone: 0131 225 4442   website: <u>www.browns-restaurant.co.uk</u>

"Favourable verdict"

It throws up all sorts of challenges when a judge gives you forty minutes to have your lunch.

The legal lord in question had throughout the case that had taken me from the north-east to Edinburgh, appeared a friendly enough chap.

He was actively engaging with the legal teams and the witnesses, asking some pointed questions and expressing – as only judges can – his extreme displeasure at certain requests from the advocates that represented the contesting parties.

His direction that lunch was shorter than normal was met with alarm. None of the lawyers I know do short lunches.

Not helping either was that this case was not being heard in the Court of Session on the Royal Mile where there are legions of small restaurants able to knock up lunch in minutes.

This case was instead in a somewhat non-descript building in George Street, an area famed for eateries that service the Charlotte Square and Queen Street set with the long lunches that they seem to enjoy.

What to do then? Well in any crisis there's always a simple solution – ask a woman. That's exactly what I did, and thanks to the court's security officer I found myself in **Browns** – a charming restaurant directly opposite the court building.

Her recommendation was simple and to the point: "It's where the Edinburgh ladies do lunch."

She was 100% correct. The place was literally filled with Edinburgh's ladies doing lunch. Their chat – or was it gossip? – filled the air in a restaurant that from the outside looks small but which opens up into a cavern once inside, complete with trees. It has a distinct Italian touch.

So would **Browns** be able to respond to the challenges of Lord McGhie? More than ably I am delighted to report – and it also served up a pretty mean lunch in those forty minutes too.

Blackboards high in the ceiling showed the specials, while the menu was filled with life's simple treasures such as duck, trout and other fishy things, steaks, burgers, chicken and salads.

My needs were simple. A starter and a main course.

With summer still to arrive and a distinct chill in the Edinburgh air, I opted for the soup of the day, a rich and thick tomato option that hit all the right spots and came served with the obligatory bun and butter.

Main course had to be something that was quick so the pasta and lamb with a creamy

mustard sauce from the specials board was ordered.

The resultant dish was obviously Edinburgh's version of stovies, except the tatties were pasta and the beef replaced with lamb.

The pasta was just right, but the lamb was somewhat conspicuous by its absence in any great quantity. Then again, did I really expect a great amount of it given the retail price of lamb at the butcher and in the supermarket?

It proved an interesting forty minutes as I surveyed the surroundings. The Edinburgh ladies, with their various gold adornments and jewels, were chatting over their large glasses of white wine. Surely the credit crunch lay behind the lack of champagne, which appeared on the menu on numerous occasions in all different varieties and at various prices.

The staff too were dashing back and forth making sure every whim was catered for. I must say they did look rather smart in their uniforms.

With lunch, a bottle of sparkling water and a refreshing pot of tea consumed inside thirty minutes, **Browns** more than met Lord McGhie's instruction.

The biggest problem, however, was that the waiting staff appeared unwilling to return to the table so I could pay the bill. This must be an Edinburgh thing as other diners lingered after receiving their bill, some even ordering more drink.

In any case I had work to do and went searching for a waitress so I could return to the court for an afternoon of stimulating discussions. Staff could have been a little more attentive.

Oh, and one issue. With Edinburgh's main streets a war zone because of the construction of the £100million tram system, there are parking problems in George Street and Charlotte Square area. At least you will be able to walk off lunch – or dinner – afterwards.

Quality of Food	5
Menu Choice	5
Surroundings	5
Location	4
Service	3
Value for Money	4
Total *[out of 30]*	**26**

Dakota Forth Bridge
South Queensferry, Edinburgh

telephone: 0870 423 4293   website: www.dakotaforthbridge.co.uk

"Stylish setting for the perfect steak"

For those who travel to Edinburgh regularly there have been two multimillion-pound construction projects to watch in recent months.

The new spur from the Forth Road Bridge to link into the motorway system at Newbridge, on the outskirts of the capital, has proved a boon since its opening at the start of October.

But far more interesting has been the creation of the large, black glass palace beside the bridge by entrepreneurial Scots hotelier Ken McCulloch.

The **Dakota** Hotel was always going to be different and it has been fascinating to see it take shape while travelling through the roadworks at a snail's pace heading to Edinburgh or, conversely, queuing to get through the bridge tolls to head back north.

What I can say is that the **Dakota's** somewhat different exterior is more than matched by an interior which is stylish and chic in the extreme.

The roof space of the reception area – and bar and grill – is akin to the set from a *Star Wars* movie, with the air-conditioning ducts and the metalwork that carries the electrical wiring and lights hanging loose. No false ceiling here to hide the necessities.

The extensive woodwork in the restaurant includes the floor, the window blinds and, for want of a better expression, the lattice fence that screens it off into different areas.

The central feature is an amazing display of wine, the influence for which is drawn, I suspect, from the main restaurant in the Columbus Hotel in Monaco developed by Mr McCulloch and F1 racing driver David Coulthard.

It has to be said that my visit was designed to test the **Dakota**. I arrived just after 2pm, the point when many heathen restaurants shut their doors and turn customers away. Not so the **Dakota**; it welcomed me with open arms.

The menu was simple, but matched the surroundings – chic and oh so with-it.

The emphasis is on fresh, seasonal food, particularly seafood. It was a surprise to see oysters – and even more delightful to read about the seafood platter, which includes a half lobster, a quarter brown crab, two oysters, six mussels, six surf clams, one scallop, one razor clam and two langoustines.

But what made me really salivate was the steak tartare. Wonderfully courageous for Scotland, but more – for me, at least – a dinner delight than lunch.

That I'd eaten very little other than seafood – and some of it raw – in the previous ten days left me focusing on what Scotland does best – beef, and preferably medium rare. That said, I could have selected from chicken, cod, lemon sole or gnocchi.

With the main course chosen, it was to the starters that I then turned – smoked salmon with blinis, old-fashioned pork terrine with piccalilli, seared tuna salad and roasted cashew nuts, potted shrimps or dressed brown crab and a langoustine cocktail, to name but some.

The cold day necessitated something warming. Here, the **Dakota** did exceptionally well with its fish and shellfish soup, which came with its own jar of grated Parmesan cheese and walnut toast with a chilli mayonnaise.

The beef – an aged rib-eye – was cooked to perfection, wonderfully seared to retain the flavour and all the juices. Each bite melted in the mouth.

It came with a Béarnaise sauce, itself something of a challenge to create given that if too hot, it curdles, and if too cold, it does not properly thicken.

Thin-cut chips were served with the rib-eye, but not on the plate. They came, creatively, in their own can, complete with chip paper.

The green salad I ordered as a side dish was not the assortment of different leaves, including the dreaded roquette, that is served up by some. Instead, it was whole, chunky lettuce leaves that had been tossed in a vinaigrette, judging by the taste.

Cheese and oatcakes, complete with a pot of tea, rounded off lunch. But here was my only disappointment.

The trendy nature of the place means that it creates its own oatcakes. They weren't to my liking, not just because they did not look like traditional oatcakes, nor taste like them. Rather, they were so hard and crunchy they were in danger of breaking one's teeth.

The cheese could also have benefited from being left to breathe for a couple of hours longer. It appeared to have come straight from the fridge.

That said, these were the only negative points from my visit.

The staff were wonderful and very attentive. But then I was the only person brave enough to venture out for lunch post the 2pm Scottish watershed.

Dakota isn't exactly the cheapest. It's also not the sort of place you are likely to nip out to if you stay north of Perth. Still, it's somewhere nice if you are near the capital – or stuck in traffic at the bridge.

Quality of Food	4
Menu Choice	5
Surroundings	5
Location	4
Service	4
Value for Money	4
Total *[out of 30]*	**26**

The Dome
14 George Street, Edinburgh

telephone: 0131 624 8624   website: <u>www.thedomeedinburgh.com</u>

"Not bad, by all accounts"

I was feeling faint, so we descended into **The Dome's** rear garden café, on Edinburgh's Rose Street, for a cold drink.

In the heat of a summer's day, we had been pounding the lengths of Princes Street, Rose Street and George Street searching for those elusive designer bargains.

But that's not why I felt ill – I'd just seen some of the outrageous prices in Harvey Nichols. Only a footballer's wife would have been laughing all the way to the bank after a spending spree in there!

So that's how we came to be sitting in the back garden of what used to be a bank.

In 1843, the Commercial Bank of Scotland paid £20,000 for what was the old Physicians' Hall on George Street. They promptly knocked it down and built the outstanding Graeco-Roman building which stands today. It has been trading as a bar and restaurant for a decade.

It is a magnificent building, with arched and keystoned windows, a six-columned Corinthian portico, carved pedimental sculptures and original marble columns and mosaic floors inside.

Aesculapius, the God of Healing is embossed on the bronze entrance doors. Through them, there is an enormous crystal chandelier, twin staircases with gilded balusters flanking the magnificent telling hall, arched ceilings and a coffered central dome.

When in Edinburgh, it is always under this majestic dome that we have lunch, not just to admire the former bank's architecture – but also to treat ourselves to their exquisite luncheon menu.

But on this occasion, we had booked a table in **The Dome's** Grill Room, so we could invest some time on the à la carte evening menu.

The Grill Room has crisp, white linen and sparkling silverware with an atmosphere to match. Jeans or black tie are acceptable attire, and due to the sheer size of the place, you feel relaxed immediately.

There are always plenty of impeccably presented staff buzzing about, and there's never much of a wait for a drink or a menu.

So, putting my money where my mouth is, on to the food.

The starters arrived quickly – duck liver pâté with kumquat marmalade and toasted brioche for my shopping partner, and the plum tomato and buffalo mozzarella salad with balsamic shallots and asparagus spears for me.

We debated the merits of a kumquat, and decided that the marmalade was never going to live up to the excellent violet version he had on holiday, when it was served with pâté de foie gras.

However, **The Dome** pâté was described as "creamy" and the marmalade "tangy".

My salad was OK, but a little overdressed for my liking. And I prefer beef tomatoes with mozzarella, but that's just me.

Both starters were adequate, but not historic. Perhaps we were being too picky – food critics are prone to this, you know.

I should point out that presentation on both accounts was of a very high standard.

On to the main event, and it was a vegetable Balti for me, with sticky Jasmine rice and garlic naan bread. The rice was delicately flavoured – and very sticky – but the curry sauce was a bit hot for my palate. The vegetables could have been more exciting.

Trouble is, there's so much more to admire under **The Dome** that the food almost comes second place.

The meat-eater decided on the roast breast of chicken to follow his pâté. It was topped with Parma ham and mozzarella, and served with sautéed new potatoes, green beans, sun blushed tomatoes and a basil dressing.

High marks were given for presentation and taste, but he didn't clean the plate.

Perhaps he was saving himself for dessert. We were banking on the menu being mouthwatering, and we were not wrong.

The Dome's sticky toffee pudding had to be put to the test and was deemed "delicious", dripping with coconut ice cream and topped with flaked, toasted coconut.

I chose from the selection of sorbets and Italian ice creams because my mouth was still on fire. Perfect.

The wine menu was steep in terms of price, but easily narrowed down to a bottle of house Pinot Grigio delle Venezie.

Quality of Food	3
Menu Choice	4
Surroundings	5
Location	5
Service	5
Value for Money	4
Total [out of 30]	**26**

Hadrian's, The Balmoral
1 Princes Street, Edinburgh

telephone: 0131 556 2414   website: www.thebalmoralhotel.com

"And at number one . . ."

We were in Edinburgh and a gaggle of girls at the table next to us were all dressed in pink, from their fingernails down to their trainers.

It wasn't a fashion statement – they were getting in the mood for the MoonWalk, a charity walk taking place that night which would see thousands power-walking either a 'half moon' or a 'full moon' marathon around the city wearing bras.

"Just their bras?" my husband inquired.

I said I didn't think so.

Galoshes might have been more appropriate given the weather, but the walk still managed to raise a respectable £2.5million for breast cancer research. Good work, girls.

To get to Edinburgh from Aberdeen, we had decided to take the train. En route, the guard announced a reminder that the service was non-smoking, "which includes anyone currently hanging out of the window".

Laughter rippled down the aisles, but it was a reminder of this modern era – and a stark contrast to the old-fashioned first-class carriage in which we were travelling.

The train was evocative of the grand old days when opulence and sophistication were in vogue. It gave us a taste for the finer things in life, which was fortunate as we were heading for The Balmoral, at 1 Princes Street.

Adjacent to Waverley Station, The Balmoral has a magnificent clock tower, and the time is always set two minutes fast so people don't miss their trains.

With no time to waste, I finally made it on to the red carpet and was lost for words. Not because I had just scaled the Waverley Steps – it was the sheer grandeur of

Edinburgh's historic landmark hotel that took my breath away.

This is one of Rocco Forte's hotels, whose collection includes Hotel Savoy in Florence and Brown's Hotel in London.

A member of The Leading Hotels of the World, it's the kind of place where you have coffee in the drawing room, afternoon tea accompanied by a harpist, or a glass or three of bubbly at Scotland's only Bollinger Bar.

Carpeted steps lead to a smart doorman, who waves you in and says "welcome back". Inside, it's pure luxury, with glass domes, a grand staircase and Venetian chandeliers. Sumptuous suites six floors up have the best views of the castle, the Scott Monument and Princes Street.

Hadrian's, the hotel's brasserie which faces on to North Bridge, is the epitome of Art Deco style. The decor is reminiscent of dark chocolate and fresh mint leaves. Walnut floors and crisp, white tablecloths provide a chic, relaxed ambience.

Jeff Bland, The Balmoral's Michelin-starred chef, created the à la carte menu with its eclectic mix of Scottish and European dishes.

We found it quite a challenge to come to a decision on food. Fortunately, the MoonWalkers provided a welcome interruption from the serious business of choosing.

The wine menu covers a wide range of tastes from around the globe, but Pouilly Fumé, Domaine Jean Claude Chatelain was a winner.

Amuses-bouche of seared scallops arrived unexpectedly and served as an exciting taste of what was to follow.

We passed on starters as we find it difficult (these days) to force down pudding as well. If I had had the stamina, the snow pea, asparagus soup with a hint of ginger and coriander sounded tempting.

So it was straight to the mains and, for me, orecchiette (little ears) pasta with four cheese and pancetta sauce, which can be had as a starter or main course – I greedily chose the latter. The pasta shells tasted fresh and the sauce was as it should be: thick, creamy, chunky.

For the birthday boy – the reason behind our special trip – it had to be Scottish traditional fillet steak from the grill menu with a sauce Béarnaise from the sauce menu (served separately) and a side order of chunky fries. He reported that his steak was absolutely delicious, and I can vouch for the fries.

Suffice to say in a restaurant of this quality, the service and attention to detail are second to none. The staff were friendly and efficient in that expertly trained manner of not being too intrusive.

A Muscat crème brulée with crystallised fruits was the icing on the proverbial cake for me, while opposite, a plate of fresh strawberries with blackcurrant white wine sauce and vanilla pod ice cream was the real show stopper – simply and brilliantly done.

After dinner, I was lost for words again. The hotel's glamorous Bollinger Bar is the ultimate indulgence with its extensive collection of vintage champagne and resident jazz pianist.

For a special occasion, The Balmoral rolls out the red carpet in style.

Quality of Food	5
Menu Choice	4
Surroundings	5
Location	5
Service	5
Value for Money	4
Total [out of 30]	**28**

Malmaison

1 Tower Place, Leith, Edinburgh

telephone: 0131 468 5000   website: www.malmaison-edinburgh.co.uk

"Capital cuisine"

The sunshine on Leith was deliciously warming as it streamed through the windows of the bus jiggling its way across Edinburgh.

It was a bumpy journey as it appeared every road between Princes Street and the Shore had been dug up to make way for the new tram system which is due to be launched in a few years.

Having been tipped off by a friendly local that taxis were taking, on average, three times longer to complete a journey since the roadworks began, I thought I'd catch a bus instead to my destination, the **Malmaison** Hotel, in Leith.

Travelling by bus was a great way to see the sights, and a good way of ensuring that I arrived in time to meet my dinner companion feeling relaxed and refreshed, instead of being grumpy at having had to fork out a small fortune on a cab ride.

The bus stop is just a few minutes' walk from the **Malmaison**, a boutique hotel perched on the banks of the River Forth. Outside the hotel, there's a nice terraced area where you can enjoy food and drinks while watching boats bobbing up and down on the river.

It may only be a short hop away

from the city centre, yet it feels miles away, and rather continental.

Sitting outside gave my friend and I the chance to get a proper look at the actual building, a lovely old riverside property with a central clock tower and lots of period features.

It has, according to legend, seen quite a few colourful goings-on over the years and, in its time, has been a seamen's mission and a house of ill-repute for ladies of the night. But things have changed – I couldn't see any sailors and silently prayed my friend and I wouldn't be mistaken for the latter.

We were dining in the brasserie, which has the look and atmosphere of a generations-old Parisian bistro.

With dark flooring, lots of ironwork lit by candlelight, wooden chairs and leather banquettes, it feels cosy and romantic. The choice of decor is not accidental – while the great French general, Napoleon, was away, his lover, Josephine, was at play, creating Château de Malmaison, a love nest for her all-conquering lover to return to.

The story goes that the diminutive despot was none too chuffed that Josephine had spent his recently acquired fortune on giving a house a spectacular makeover.

Malmaison hotels, bars and brasseries aim to carry on where Josephine left off and, to an extent, it works – there's definitely plenty of entente cordiale about the place.

Having been shown to a table for two by a helpful maître d', we were immediately presented with a jug of iced water and a basket filled with warm crusty bread, butter and a pesto-based dip.

We opted for food from the home-grown and local menu, which offered a choice of four starters, mains and sweets.

Head chef Matt Powell takes great care to use local producers and each side of the menu carries a brief history of each, along with contact details.

A starter of warm Scottish asparagus, Planeta olive oil and local cheesemonger Ian Mellis's goat's gouda sounded too good to resist, and as it has such a short season, we both plumped for this.

Asparagus has a delicate flavour and really doesn't like to be messed with – this was ideal. The oil and sweet goat's cheese topping was light enough to let the mild taste of the vivid green stems come bounding through.

Main course choices were: Finnan haddie fishcake; creamed crowdie goat's cheese polenta; penne pasta with Crombie's Lombardy sausage and tomato, or at an extra cost, Buccleuch rump beef olives with a red onion mash.

My meat-eating side couldn't resist the beef olives, while my guest, who had good local knowledge, said Crombie's sausages were famous so immediately plumped for the pasta dish.

Meanwhile, we had ordered a bottle of house Merlot and some sparkling water, which gave the waitress the green light to offer to top up our glasses after every other sip. Still, better to have over-attentive staff than be ignored, I say.

The beef olives, stuffed with sausage meat, literally melted in the mouth, as the rump was cooked to tender perfection. The red onion mash – soft, creamy spuds with a strong, but not overpowering, onion flavour – went down a treat. The gravy, which had hints of red wine and herbs, got ten out of ten for texture and flavour.

The enormous bowl of penne pasta would have kept an Olympic athlete happy. The pasta, smothered in a flavour-packed sweet tomato sauce, had a nice bite and included lots of chunks of Lombardy sausage, a fantastically pungent chorizo-style sausage that had my guest making lots of "mmmm" sounds.

After what we considered to be a dignified period, we took a look at the dessert menu, which offered

Eton mess with Brammle liqueur; organic lemon drizzle cake with Rowan Glen crème fraîche; mango panna cotta with mango salsa, and Anster cheese from Ian Mellis served with walnut bread and rhubarb chutney.

My chum was drawn to the panna cotta, a deliciously light and creamy pud with a bright, sunshine-yellow, tangy salsa which she reluctantly let me taste. I, grudgingly, let her try the crumbly white, very moreish, melt-in-the-mouth Anster cheese and walnut bread.

At the time of writing, **Malmaison** is set to open a hotel in Aberdeen on the site formerly occupied by the Queen's Hotel. If the service and food there are as good as the Edinburgh hotel, it will be a cool and stylish addition to the Aberdeen dining scene.

Quality of Food	4
Menu Choice	4
Surroundings	5
Location	5
Service	5
Value for Money	4
Total [out of 30]	**27**

The Doll's House Restaurant

3 Church Square, St Andrews

telephone: 01334 477422   website: www.dolls-house.co.uk

"The Doll's House playing a stormer"

We were off to dine at **The Doll's House**. No, not with miniature cups and saucers filled with imaginary tea which had to be drunk while making polite conversation with Jemima, Madeleine and Tiny Tears.

This is a proper restaurant with a somewhat unusual name, part of the group of 'house' restaurants co-owned by the husband of Scots TV star Carol Smillie and Simon Littlejohn, whose interests include Inverness restaurants The Mustard Seed and Kitchen on The River.

Tucked away in a quiet courtyard between St Andrews' two main shopping streets, **The Doll's House** occupies a quaint two-storey building with room to dine outside when the weather is fine.

Inside, the decor keeps the playroom theme with assorted toys and knick-knacks scattered around shelves and mounted on the walls. We had chosen to dine from the early evening menu and it was clearly a popular event, with almost every table occupied.

I must say straight away that the excellent value for money was not compromised by either service, surroundings or quality of food. Everything about the dining experience at **The Doll's House** was first rate – but more of that later.

The menu choice was more than adequate for a set meal. Two of the party opted for the mackerel pâté with oatcake and a horseradish cream; I chose the goat's cheese tart, and from the children's menu, the youngest member of the party decided on melon and fresh fruit. Each was declared delicious, the only complaint being the single oatcake served with each portion of pâté. The quality and quantity deserved an extra one.

For main course, I departed from my norm and chose the pork loin with a grain mustard sauce. Elsewhere, orders were placed for the haddock with a Martini and grape sauce, rump steak in a red wine and peppercorn sauce and, from the junior selection, a junior rump steak.

The star of the show was the fish – a soft, white chunk of haddock befitting the East Neuk setting, complemented perfectly by the sauce.

The pork and the steaks were by no means second-rate – quite the contrary. The red meat was perfectly pink, as requested, and the pork avoided the pitfall of being overcooked and chewy.

The portion of potatoes and vegetables served between three wasn't the largest, but fortunately we had ordered a side of fries which padded things – including our waistlines – out nicely.

Our bottle of wine, a pleasant Italian white from the house selection, matched the food choices of the grown-ups perfectly.

All the while, the youthful staff went about their business with efficiency and a smile, ensuring that the whole **Doll's House** experience was one to be remembered and, I dare say, repeated in the not too distant future.

The food was fantastic value for money which I would challenge other restaurants to match. Three adult meals, wine and a proper grown-up children's meal for a price designed to get families out to dinner.

I cannot recommend **The Doll's House** highly enough – if you're ever at the home of golf, make sure you drop by. If you only have time for lunch then so much the better – at that time of day.

If talk of St Andrews has given you the taste for a visit to the seaside town, you can celebrate all things Scottish at the end of November with the annual St Andrews Festival.

Enjoy an eclectic and colourful programme of festivities celebrating the feast day of Scotland's patron saint with the very best of the country's rich national culture and cuisine.

Highlights include traditional

and classical music concerts, dance and drama, arts and crafts exhibitions and a kite festival on the West Sands.

For more information, see: www.standrewsfestival.co.uk or telephone: 01334 475000.

Quality of Food	4
Menu Choice	5
Surroundings	4
Location	5
Service	5
Value for Money	5
Total *[out of 30]*	**28**

The Glass House Restaurant

80 North Street, St Andrews

telephone: 01334 473673   website: www.houserestaurants.com

"First, second and third time lucky"

House. House. House. It may sound like a night at the bingo, and a successful one, to boot. Place Doll's, Grill or **Glass** in front and you get the hat-trick of restaurants which form a cornerstone of the eating-out scene in St Andrews.

The Glass House sits opposite the traditional university buildings which have been turning out academics for hundreds of years. If those students ever need a lesson in how to serve up quality food at a price even they can afford, it's staring them right in the face.

From the moment you walk in it becomes clear that the owners set extremely high standards for their staff. Having already witnessed them in action at our previous house nights, their colleagues were not about to let cracks appear. With so much glass around that wouldn't be a wise move.

The early evening menu offers outstanding value, which is why we booked for 5.30pm. The other diners who filled every table on offer within an hour clearly shared our philosophy – to the point where it teetered between cosy and cramped. A minor gripe, but one worth noting should you choose to dine here.

The mouthwatering set choices are complemented by a chalk board with specials, and you can, if you wish, opt to eat from the à la carte menu.

We did a spot of mixing and matching, with number one son deciding one of the blackboard options had been invented just for him. His younger brother didn't want any of the starters on offer, but since he had decided the main course rump steak was just what he needed, we opted for the set menu for him anyway. As adults, we felt it was our duty to sample as much of the fare as we could reasonably manage.

The children shared garlic bread with mozzarella cheese for starters while we gave a trio the taste test.

My grilled field mushroom filled with mascarpone cheese, spring onions and garlic butter, and then sprinkled with a herb crumb, was

excellent – the cheese, onion and garlic filling melted and the crunchy crumb added some texture.

We shared the lemon pepper chicken and pineapple salad, while my wife declared that the smoked trout, caper and prawn salad with tomato and chive dressing was "delightful".

Full marks for the food so far.

On to the main event and our eldest seemed pleased with his choice of chicken with smoked pancetta and melted mozzarella served on a bed of tagliatelle with a tomato, garlic and oregano sauce. It was an adult portion, but it disappeared with the speed of a child being told the sweetie cupboard was no longer out of bounds.

From the set menu, we had a rump steak and fries, without its barbecue and smoked bacon sauce; spaghetti with pork and mushroom piri piri, and last, but by no means least, a salmon fillet served on a lemon, spinach, prawn and tattie stir-fry.

Did any disappoint? Not a bit of it. The steak was pink and melted in the mouth, the salmon was fresh and light and the piri piri pork spicy and tender.

The children assured us they had space left for some chocolate fudge cake and, despite the fact they looked as if they were trying to wear it by the time they were forced to give up, they insisted it was good. The few crumbs we shared between us confirmed their judgment.

Fantastic value for money for quality cooking.

This is a venue worth travelling to – the food is a cut above without a haute-cuisine price tag. The venue is relaxed, so there's no standing on ceremony, and while it can get a little cramped when full, that does nothing to take away from the experience.

There's an old saying that people in glass houses shouldn't throw stones – meaning those who are vulnerable shouldn't attack others. On this evidence, **The Glass House** can go on the offensive any time it likes.

Quality of Food	5
Menu Choice	5
Surroundings	4
Location	5
Service	4
Value for Money	5
Total *[out of 30]*	**28**

Sangster's
51 High Street, Elie

telephone: 01333 331001   website: www.sangsters.co.uk

"Simply the best" – *Michelin Star awarded in January 2009*

It is often said that the best things in life are simple.

It's obviously the philosophy followed by **Sangster's** which, based in Elie, is unquestionably one of the country's top eateries.

Owner/chef Bruce Sangster is no stranger to success and has been winning awards since his days at Perth's Murrayshall Hotel. His trophy haul includes Scottish Chef of the Year in 1989, the National Chef of the Year in 2000, many prizes in the world's annual culinary cup and British Garde d'Or National Chef.

It is, however, the unassuming and not-in-your-face nature of that success, as well as the food that he creates, which appeals.

A recent trip to the land of my ancestors allowed an evening out in the East Neuk village that, in the time of my forebears, would have had a thriving fishing industry as opposed to the holiday-home community that it now appears to have become.

But don't go there expecting a sign that bawls out **Sangster's**. You can easily go past it. We managed to twice. The first indication of a world-class restaurant is in the brass box used to display the menu beside a door that looks just like every other one in the village.

Step inside and you're in the front room of a former home where the greeter and waitress is Mr Sangster's wife, Jackie.

Pleasantries exchanged, we took a seat, ordered a swift gin and savoured the surroundings. The master could be seen at work in the kitchen, while all around the pleasantly decorated reception area were the awards he had won.

There was even a framed review from the national newspaper that made light of his sudden departure from the merchant bank where he was executive chef for nine years. That posting ended after he was sacked for passing on a 'bawdy' e-mail. He, however, won his claim for unfair and wrongful dismissal before returning home to Scotland and setting up in Fife.

The menu was simplicity itself: three starters, two intermediate courses, four mains and three desserts, including cheese.

So to the selection, which proved easy. Scallops, soup and a fillet steak for me. My dining companions set the chef a challenge with their choices.

My pan-roasted Ross-shire scallops came in a truly scrumptious coconut broth with spring onions and coriander which combined well to give that extra zing.

The others, too, were content with the crisp bon bon of duck confit and foie gras with wilted cucumber and Asian spices, along with the twice-baked cheese soufflé made with mature cheddar from the Mull of Kintyre.

Next up was the soup made with locally grown Jerusalem artichokes.

That proved a real treat on a day in which snow had stopped play at nearby St Andrews. This deliciously smooth creation was made all the better thanks to a touch of truffle oil and double cream.

If I had one regret, it was not asking my dining companions for a piece of their panko-crusted Arbroath Smokies with a mango and pineapple salsa. The fish connoisseur – well, he is, allegedly, the UK's number two in terms of promoting the fishing sector – was full of praise for this. The former Fife farmer who now ploughs a long, lonely furrow in politics was likewise impressed by the restaurant's deep-fried version of Scotland's best-known smoked fish.

Sangster's, however, saved the best for last. My fillet was, without question, one of the finest steaks I have ever had the honour of eating.

The same compliment, too, came from the pair who opted for the pan-seared fillet of North Sea halibut served on a bed of gratin potatoes and nutty Dutch cabbage with caraway seeds in a creamy shellfish sauce. Not only did it look good, but the combination of flavours worked well with the halibut, which was cooked beautifully.

The long-suffering wife of my fishing friend went for the medallions of venison loin with a mushroom gratin, red cabbage and apple compote, and gratin potatoes with a red wine sauce. It, too, proved a real treat.

We washed dinner down with the house Sauvignon Blanc.

There being no room left for desserts, we opted for the teas and coffees and marvelled at this culinary treasure in a part of rural Scotland.

The dining-room was made all the better by the paintings of local scenes. I never asked if they were for sale or not, but there was one of the picturesque harbour at St Monans, home to my great-grandmother, that I took an immediate liking to.

I've long been told the best things in life come fae Fife. Now I can believe it.

Quality of Food	5
Menu Choice	5
Surroundings	5
Location	4
Service	5
Value for Money	5
Total *[out of 30]*	**29**

Rococo

48 West Regent Street, Glasgow

telephone: 0141 221 5004   website: www.rococoglasgow.co.uk

"Melt in the mouth style and class"

Across the north and north-east of Scotland, I always find the choice and quality of eateries as good as anything the rest of the country has to offer.

So it came as little surprise when *EatScotland* recently announced its inaugural silver award winners that a string of restaurants in the area were recognised.

From the top-class Three Chimneys in Skye to Ballater's Green Inn and the excellent Castleton House Hotel, near Glamis, high standards are being set constantly.

All three were among the forty-two establishments acknowledged, but the inclusion of several central belt restaurants roused my curiosity.

With a trip to Glasgow pencilled into my diary already, I took the opportunity to see what they had to offer.

One of those celebrating its silver award was **Rococo**, located in the heart of the city centre on West George Street.

With a kitchen led by head chef Mark Tamburrini, the place has a reputation for good food in stylish surroundings at reasonable prices.

Within moments of arriving, we could see why.

Rococo's decor doesn't follow

129

any theme in particular, but is undoubtedly classy, which lends itself to the restaurant being an appropriate venue for any manner of gathering.

A twenty-first birthday party was in full flow on one side, but we barely noticed it, seated as we were in another room just a few yards away.

With beautiful lilies hanging delicately over each table, subtle lighting and strains of Billie Holiday playing gently in the background, the atmosphere was relaxed and romantic.

The dinner menu is based largely on Tamburrini's liking for modern Scottish cooking, with French and Italian influences.

After a delightful king prawn amuse-bouche, I chose a Scottish smoked salmon papillote for my starter, which was served with lemon crème fraîche, poached langoustine and a caviar and chive dressing.

Beautifully presented, the sharp combination of flavours bounced around the plate in a pleasingly frisky fashion.

My dining companion chose boudin of chicken, which was served with crispy veal sweetbreads, shallot cream and a smoked bacon jus, which made the dish a rich and tasty experience.

Our main courses, washed down with a fruity bottle of Beaumont Chenin Blanc, were just as well-received.

The waiter told me that my cannon of Perthshire lamb was a fattier cut than normal, and this did prove to be the case, but it was cooked to perfection and the juicy tender lamb was delicious. The layered tian of aubergine and courgette which accompanied it was an unexpected masterstroke as the vegetables melded into the homely taste of the lamb.

Across the table, the pan-roasted supreme of halibut was polished off appreciatively.

With pomme ecrassé, a tarte tatin of vine cherry tomatoes and buttered asparagus and port wine reduction, it was little wonder it was consumed at speed.

After a little time to peruse the dessert menu, we went with two long-time favourites of ours – rich sticky toffee pudding with caramel ice-cream and butterscotch sauce and a rather substantial cheese board.

While we tried, it was difficult to fault the quality of our food, so our thoughts turned elsewhere to service.

The staff were thoroughly pleasant, helpful and well-drilled on etiquette, but were a little slower than we would have liked.

The long journey south from Aberdeen perhaps didn't help, but waiting for an hour before we received our starters was not what we had anticipated.

I also believe had they picked

up the pace just a touch, we would have wandered off into the night happily contemplating what was an otherwise faultless meal.

Any time I visit Glasgow, I notice another new building or bridge as its regeneration continues and **Rococo** is typical of the smart, cosmopolitan city it has become.

As the city which surrounds it strives to improve, the incentive for the restaurant itself to keep progressing is there, too.

EatScotland's silver award winners are eligible to be considered for the first batch of gold awards and with a touch of tinkering, I'm sure **Rococo** will be among those rewarded again.

Quality of Food	5
Menu Choice	4
Surroundings	5
Location	5
Service	4
Value for Money	4
Total [out of 30]	**27**

Thai Lemongrass
24 Renfrew Street, Glasgow

telephone: 0141 331 1315   website: www.thailemongrass.net

"You are my sunshine"

It had, sadly, been one of those long, exhausting days

listening to the moans of others.

Quite why some people always believe that the world is

out to get them I have no idea.

What was clear was that those moaning hadn't spotted the opportunity in the dilemma they faced. The entrepreneur would have seen it, but this particular feather-bedded part of the Scottish business world hadn't yet realised that there is some truth in the adage that "whar's thar's muck thar's brass".

Why, you may be wondering, am I using those lines to open a restaurant review? Partly, I guess, because when I'm feeling down and need an injection of sunshine, I find the best place for it is a Thai restaurant – and in Glasgow, there is none better than the **Thai Lemongrass**.

One would think that an eatery of its calibre would be in the trendy Merchant City, as opposed to being sandwiched between some of Glasgow's 'finest' pubs on Renfrew Street and opposite the towering UGC cinema complex.

But then, as I said earlier, where there is muck there is often brass. In this case, it just happens that the **Thai Lemongrass** really is the jewel in the crown and a rare oasis of calm in the lean, mean, weegieland that is Glasgow.

I've been to the restaurant many times before and, on each occasion, left feeling that I've been to Thailand and back. There's no pandering to British tastes here, just decent and authentic Thai food that evokes, for me, many fond

memories of gorgeous dinners on a beach in Phuket as the sun set over the Andaman Sea.

Thai food, with its delicate and aromatic tastes, can however prove spicy because of the addition of chillies, so beware.

I started with the spare ribs and plum sauce – not the conventional stubby ribs that you get covered in sticky sauce in many Chinese restaurants, but lengthy chunks of meat, and oh so sweet because it is served on the bone. The sauce came in its own little dish rather than being poured over the ribs.

Next was the Tom Yum Goong seafood soup, which tasted as if it had come straight from Phuket.

This marvellous soup with shrimp and squid is served piping hot in a broth that is made from mushrooms, lemongrass, lime, hot red chillies and coriander leaves. If you like hot and sour, this has to be the perfect taste combination. But, as I say, beware the chilli, otherwise your mouth may match the heat that appeared to have given the two 'TV celebrities' who were also dining that particular evening their sun tans.

It proved an interesting evening watching and listening in to weegie-ites Colin and Justin and their two dining companions. I was delighted to see that they did not get any special treatment from restaurant staff.

I did, however, feel the need to

ask where they got their tans, but then bottled it.

I guess I'll never know where they came by their complexions. Was it à la Tommy Sheridan in a tanning booth in Sauchiehall Street, some tropical location overseas, a bottle, or just from too much exposure? I'll leave you, dear reader, to decide.

Back, however, to food and away from the diversion of the Z lists.

My main course was an absolute taste sensation. I love fish, but this was sea bass as I had never before eaten it, not even in Thailand.

It was served with the whole fish filleted, the meaty chunks extracted from it and battered, and then the most delicious Thai salad served on top.

It seemed such a shame to have to destroy this perfectly constructed creation, but then that's what I am being paid for.

The taste simply exploded in my mouth. Wow. There was the sea bass, and then there was the lime – but not just any lime. This dish had Kaffir lime leaves as well as delicately cut little cubes of lime all the way through it. What a taste, what a dinner.

To round off and clean my palate, I had the coconut ice cream.

Yes, it was expensive just for one, but you could also argue that I had been transported from Glasgow to Phuket and back in the space of two hours.

Colin and Justin were still talking with their companions as I left. Would I ask the question that I had been battling with all evening? Not on your life as I'd decided by then that if that's what too much exposure under the TV lights does to you then I will be sticking to writing.

Quality of Food	5
Menu Choice	5
Surroundings	5
Location	4
Service	5
Value for Money	4
Total *[out of 30]*	**28**

Il Padrino Ristorante

Station Square, Brora

telephone: 01408 622011

"Mamma mia!"

Just occasionally you go into a restaurant and say wow at first sight, without even sampling the food.

Il Padrino, in Brora's Station Square, certainly falls into that category for me.

I had spotted it the previous evening as I headed north up the A9 towards Caithness.

Its bright lights made me do a double take. Surely not an Italian restaurant in Brora, until now only noted really for that oh so wonderful Capaldi's ice cream?

As I returned south from a very dismal day in Caithness,

Il Padrino was just the tonic I needed to cheer me up. The warm greeting I got when I inquired of the youthful, and very enthusiastic, staff if they could feed a weary traveller on his way south to Stirling was, "Most certainly, let me show you to a table, and would you like something to drink?"

It reminded me so much of Valentino's, a one-time favourite Italian restaurant which, when it started out, was in the middle of nowhere at Durno, between Pitcaple and Inverurie. It has since moved to the Garioch capital and lost some of its rural charm, in my eyes.

Il Padrino opened in the spring and certainly appears to have got the support of the folk of Brora.

There were only two other diners in it when I arrived just after 7pm that particular Friday evening.

By the time I left, it was packed, boosted by a rather large group of adults and teenagers, along with a German family and four elderly chaps who not only liked Italian food, but their red wine, too. To add to the mix were locals who came in to order their takeaways.

The teenagers on the large group table were into pizzas. I don't quite get pizza, it has to be said, and nowadays avoid it, regardless of where it comes from or who cooks it.

My first choice for a starter – the insalata di mare, seafood marinated in the best olive oils and vinegar, served on a bed of leaves – was not available. The waitress was full of apologies.

She need not have been as I was actually rather glad, in hindsight, that there was no seafood salad.

My second choice, the creamy garlic mussels from the specials board, now became my starter – and what a show-stopper they proved to be.

To say this was delicious would be an understatement. Every taste bud came alive on sampling this sauce, a rich concoction of garlic, thyme, rosemary, fish stock and cream. Benissimo! Mamma mia!

Would the main course be as good? My lamb shank was rather nice, although I would have to question where the lamb came from.

The meat was wonderfully tender, but lacked any real flavour of lamb. It certainly did not taste like the ones that roam the hillsides of Sutherland and thrive on heather to give them a very distinctive flavour.

That said, the roasted vegetables were rather nice. The potato mash was, however, just a little soggy for me.

I shouldn't have had a dessert, but did. The fruits of the forest cream cake went down rather well, although there was no mention on the menu of Brora's famous ice cream, which was something of a disappointment.

Il Padrino is rather tastefully decorated with its wooden floor, wood panelling and chunky tables and chairs. It's clean and warm.

The menu has all the usuals you would expect of an Italian restaurant, and all dishes are reasonably priced.

The specials board that particular night included garlic sardines, crayfish cocktail and fresh oysters for starters.

Mains from the specials stretched to grilled tuna in a lemon caper sauce, filleto rossini (a fillet steak with a creamy mushroom and Marsala wine sauce) and veal.

I was impressed particularly with the attentiveness of the young and cheery staff, who were quite happy to chat to a weary traveller.

There were some nice touches, too, including the bruschetta served at the start of my meal.

Quality of Food	4
Menu Choice	5
Surroundings	5
Location	4
Service	5
Value for Money	4
Total [out of 30]	**27**

The Anderson

Union Street, Fortrose, by Inverness

telephone: 01381 620 236   website: www.theanderson.co.uk

"International flavour"

Gordon Ramsay's latest rant has been a demand that chefs should only cook with local, seasonal foodstuffs.

The words pot and kettle spring to mind as it's been revealed his own restaurants serve food from thousands of miles away.

While I confess to liking Gordon's idea of using fresh seasonal produce whenever possible – I refuse to eat strawberries in the middle of winter – I'm certainly not upset at the thought of eating food which comes from more than a stone's throw away.

Which is perhaps just as well,

because the fare on offer at **The Anderson** in Fortrose is truly global.

This lovely old black and white building sits on Cathedral Square, slap bang in the centre of the picturesque fishing village on the Black Isle.

From the outside, it looks like the sort of place where you'd expect a nice but safe menu, the sort of eatery where high teas and Sunday roasts are the norm.

Instead American hosts, Anne and Jim Anderson, have created an eclectic menu which brings together some of their favourite foods from across the world, creating in the process a wee international oasis where foodies come to quench their thirst.

But it wasn't the menu which caught our eye as we walked into the hotel's reception hall — it was the impressive array of whiskies which lined the picture-rail height shelving.

The Anderson, which also has a cosy whisky bar and firelit country pub, carries more than 200 single-malt whiskies, many difficult to find elsewhere, as well as cask ale and the largest collection of Belgian beers in Scotland — ninety at the last count.

As a result it was named CAMRA Pub of the Year last year. But that's not the only accolade it's picked up. Executive chef Anne, an Italian-American and veteran of the New Orleans restaurant scene who moved to the Highlands five years ago, picked up a bronze award in the prestigious Scottish Chef Awards 2008.

The fifty-seater restaurant has clearly been designed by someone with a sense of fun. There's a real mixture of styles and objets d'art, ranging from a collection of original radios piled high atop a display cabinet, to giant lampshades which look homemade.

Owner Jim welcomed us and showed us to our table, explaining that the menu was changed daily and he hoped we'd find something interesting on there.

I certainly did. From a selection of ten starters, my eyes were immediately drawn to something called Tony Soprano's flamin' sausages and prawns. I love *The Sopranos* and anything that gets me closer to the mobster boss gets my vote.

After much debate about why French black pudding would be used instead of the Highland variety, my companion plumped for Gallic black pudding, served with a rich chickpea casserole and grilled flatbread.

With a cheery cry of: "Mind your eyebrows" Jim set my starter alight as he brought it to the table. Very dramatic – apparently this is the way they serve it in Fort Lee.

It wasn't huge, just one fennel sausage cut into chunks and four fat prawns. But it was mighty fine, especially the sausage which had a delicious pungency which rattled the tastebuds but slightly overwhelmed the delicate prawns which were a tad dry.

The Gallic-v-Gaelic black pudding debate was won by the French after it was declared the pudding had the nicest texture and richest flavour ever tasted. The chickpea casserole added a nuttiness to proceedings while the flatbread soaked up the juices.

For mains I plumped for tournedos of Scotch beef fillet, while the black pud convert requested a Greek-style Scotch lamb shank.

These came with a massive bowl containing a mixture of fresh vegetables including wee roast spuds, broccoli and carrots, all with that lovely hand-made look and al-dente crunch.

My beautifully cooked fillet, medium-rare as ordered, came with mushrooms and a decadent, rich blue cheese sauce that I'm sure Anne could make a fortune selling on its own. The meat was tender and while I wouldn't normally eat blue cheese and red meat together, it was a knockout combination.

Across the table, conversation was replaced by whimpers of joy, as my guest revelled in the tenderness of the sweet lamb which was doing its best to fall off the bone. Served with a mild garlic mash and fruity red wine gravy, it was quite simply, pure pleasure on a plate.

After making a deal to have a walk around the village to work off the excesses of our dinner, we ordered dessert. White chocolate crème brûlée for me and rhubarb crumble with Drambuie custard for her.

These went down a storm. I don't know how she did it, but Anne managed to make the custard taste like a large, sweet but powerful dram of the variety that should be drunk slowly in front of a roaring fire. Much nicer than the custard my old school dinner lady served.

As for the brûlée, it was so creamy and white I think Anne must have the Milky Bar kid working as a sous chef.

Quality of Food	5
Menu Choice	4
Surroundings	4
Location	4
Service	5
Value for Money	5
Total [out of 30]	**27**

Bùlas at The Ballachulish Hotel
Ballachulish

telephone: 01855 811 606   website: www.ballachulishhotel.com

"Perfect start to new year"

I have discovered the perfect antidote to Christmas in the doldrums. Hogmanay – in the Highlands.

More specifically, dinner at **Bùlas bar and bistro** at The Ballachulish Hotel, south of Fort William.

We were staying at the Lodge On The Loch Hotel, Onich, but because its restaurant was closed until February, we had been booked in for dinner at the Ballachulish, a charming, lochside hotel.

Coming from Aberdeenshire, we had to cross mountain and river, via Braemar, the busy ski slopes of Glenshee, Pitlochry and the Drumochter Pass. But we found the snow-lined, country roads to the west coast better maintained than any commuter route into Aberdeen and the journey was a pleasant aperitif.

When we arrived at the restaurant, they weren't expecting us, as the reservation hadn't been confirmed, but nevertheless, we were given a very warm welcome.

As we waited for the bagpipe player to pipe the residents into the dining-room, we enjoyed a complimentary drink by the fireside while the staff laid another table for two.

139

We perused the **Bùlas** menu, which notes that the chef has worked with suppliers to eliminate modified ingredients and that every care is taken to ensure all products and ingredients used derive from a sustainable resource, either wild or farmed responsibly.

The restaurant opened in February, 2005, and has already won the Hotel Review Scotland Food Innovation Award.

Bùlas is named after traditional Gaelic pots and the restaurant is famous for its hearty Highland dishes, perfect for sharing and feasting with friends. The Fisherman's Bùlas, for example, is the most popular and contains mussels, haddock, shrimp, scallops, fresh and smoked salmon, light wine and coriander sauce and langoustines.

Bùlas has an exciting choice of food and wine, served all day, every day.

Bookings are essential, though.

But this was no ordinary day – it was New Year's Eve and we were presented with the Hogmanay Dinner menu.

A quiet supper was not to be, however. We had unwittingly stumbled upon a fantastic Hogmanay party.

In fact, it was war. Staff took on guests with party pea-shooters while hundreds of those crazy, screaming balloons whizzed around the room. You could shoot a stranger in the back of the head and they'd turn around laughing!

Party-poppers, crackers and Christmas music filled the air.

Best of all, the staff were enjoying themselves as much as everyone else – yet not once did the service falter. This was Highland hospitality at its best.

Operations director David McAree made sure of that. He was the star of the show. If you've been to Craigellachie or Gleneagles, you'll know him.

And from the appetisers to the coffee and fudge, the quality of fare throughout was unforgettable.

Feast your eyes on the Hogmanay Dinner menu:

Assiette of home-cured salmon or confit duck rillette, followed by leek and potato soup with smoked salmon, crème fraîche and chives.

Then a glass of pink grapefruit and rosemary granite (crushed ice) to refresh the palate, followed by a choice of four mains: baked codling fillet with herb crust, grilled corn-fed chicken with Provençale tomato, saddle of lamb stuffed with Stornoway black pudding or asparagus and baby leek risotto.

To finish, iced raspberry roulade with chocolate clotted cream, followed by coffee and home-made fudge.

I can tell you now it was the finest dinner I had the fortune to experience throughout 2005. And that's saying something.

The leek and potato soup got top marks overall for flavour and consistency. The risotto, with shaved Parmesan and coriander cream, was perfect. And the fondant potato and honeyed parsnip which accompanied the saddle of slow-baked lamb was so out-of-this-world that my partner couldn't help sharing.

A bottle of fine French Champagne Mansard Brut disappeared all too quickly.

So overwhelmed were we by the welcome, excellent service and good food, we almost forgot to look at the surroundings. But you can see from the outside what to expect inside this beautiful establishment.

We strolled back across the bridge over Loch Leven, returning to the lodge to see in the New Year. Its new owners, from Singapore, fell in love with Scotland, buying the hotel for its dramatic views of Loch Linnhe and the mountains beyond.

The small group assembled in the bar had all come to get away from it all and champagne flowed like water into the early hours. Eventually, the sun came up on 2006 and the glorious view was revealed.

The job this week of untangling Christmas-tree lights and wrestling them back into boxes that need to be twice the size was made all the more enjoyable with memories of a remarkable Hogmanay on the west coast. This year, I suggest you do exactly the same.

Quality of Food	5
Menu Choice	5
Surroundings	4
Location	5
Service	5
Value for Money	4
Total *[out of 30]*	**28**

Contrast Brasserie

Ness Bank, Inverness

telephone: 01463 227889   website: www.glenmoristontownhouse.com

"Contrast hits right shade"

Inverness is booming. That's the message coming loud and clear from the Millennium city.

And as it grows, so a more cosmopolitan air creeps in and it begins to feel less like a large Highland town and more like a dynamic modern city in its own right.

The eyes of the nation turned to the north capital when Gordon Ramsay filmed one of the episodes for his *Kitchen Nightmares* series at the Glenmoriston Town House Hotel and the effects of that are still being felt.

Not least in the latest venture by

Barry Larsen and the team behind the award-winning Abstract at the Glenmoriston.

Having created the fine dining experience there, they've turned their attention to establishing a brasserie alongside, with dishes from around the world but aiming for affordable prices in a bright, buzzy atmosphere, as a contrast.

Which would explain the name of their latest eaterie, **Contrast**, which also sits on the banks of the Ness.

Armed with all this information, I was looking forward to sampling what was on offer and seeing if it could live up to its promise.

They do a two-course business lunch and also have a pre-theatre menu, which all sounds very reasonable, but we decided to go à la carte.

It does have a beautiful location on the Ness and there are plenty of tables set up outside, although this was perhaps a little too optimistic for the evening we chose. However, there is a section from the barbecue on the menu which I can imagine would be fantastic given the right weather.

Inside has an oriental feel with its dark wood floors, thoughtfully-placed screens and slat-backed chairs. I'm not sure how the crocodile skin tables fit in to this, but it was all very impressive.

The decor definitely makes a statement with the oversized lamp shades, elegant cutlery and luxurious drapes around the room.

The menu is quite extensive and does seem to boast an eclectic mix, as promised.

I chose the homemade sushi platter for my starter, but there were also fresh mussels and chorizo in a coconut and curry sauce, langoustine tails with tomato and mango dressing and fresh garden pea soup, as well as other goodies on offer.

My sushi was beautifully presented and delicately flavoured while the carpaccio of tuna across from me was a veritable work of art. It wouldn't have looked out of place on the walls, dotted as it was with crispy rice noodles and colourful vegetables.

But the presentation was matched by the taste as the slithers of cool tuna slid effortlessly down with the crispy noodles proving an ideal foil.

Meanwhile, the waitresses padded about quietly and efficiently, clad head to toe in black. They perhaps didn't display overwhelming charm but they did seem to know what they were doing.

For main course I'd toyed with the idea of the seven-hour slow-cooked lamb shank as I'd already realised they knew how to do things properly round these parts, but instead opted for the fish. There was a monkfish tagine or seared fillet of sea bass with lemongrass, but it was the hazelnut and rosemary crust on the baked haddock fillet that swayed me.

Again the presentation was faultless with the fish perched on mashed potatoes with a pool of Spanish pepper sauce around about. Perfectly judged, the herb and nut flavours from the crust stood out enough from the fish while the sweetness of the pepper sauce finished it off.

My dining companion chose the seafood linguine which was simple but spot-on. The creamy, buttery linguine was a great base for the scallops, mussels and king prawns.

Desserts didn't let the meal down at all. My lemon tart with its peaked French meringue was worthy of the best patisserie, while the strains of Albatross from the M&S advert were very nearly to be heard as the warm chocolate gâteaux across from me oozed out its soft centre of passion fruit while the vanilla ice cream softly melted on the side.

All in all I was terribly impressed with the food and the idea behind the new venture.

It looks great, tastes amazing and with places like this creeping on to the scene, Inverness's reputation as a top Scottish destination both to visit and to live can only go from strength to strength.

Quality of Food	5
Menu Choice	4
Surroundings	5
Location	4
Service	4
Value for Money	5
Total [out of 30]	**27**

Coul House Hotel

Contin, Ross-shire

telephone: 01997 421487   website: www.coulhousehotel.com

"Highland feast"

Contin is a tiny wee hamlet just a short hop from Strathpeffer and

a pleasant thirty-minute car drive from Inverness.

It's basically a pretty, one-street

town with not a lot to distract passers-by, so how I managed to miss the sign marking the entrance to the **Coul House Hotel** is a bit of a mystery.

Missing it once is one thing, passing it twice quite another. I blame my satnav system, better known as my sister-in-law, for paying too much attention to the spectacular scenery instead of looking out for the sign marking the hidden entrance to the hotel.

Third time lucky, we found it, and immediately found ourselves on a gorgeous sweeping driveway, the sort one could imagine being used in a Merchant Ivory period film.

At the end of the drive sits a handsome gabled mansion, complete with sweeping lawn where, occasionally, peacocks like to stroll as red kites circle lazily in the sky above.

Should you be out for a walk, it's a fantastic sight, while those enjoying a game of putting on the hotel's private course can, hand on heart, claim their game involved a birdie.

The wildlife can also be enjoyed from within the main dining-room, a gorgeous octagonal room with an eighteen foot ceiling, traditional tall fireplace and three floor-to-ceiling windows offering views across the gardens towards the Strathconon valley and the mountains beyond.

Before being shown to our table by the smartly dressed waitress, we enjoyed a pre-dinner drink, complimentary olives and a good old blether in the adjacent bar, a nice country-house-style room where residential and non-residential guests relaxed before being asked to the dining-room.

Conversation was halted, temporarily, as we studied the menu created by head chef Garry Kenley, a talented chap originally from Inverness who spent several years in America working with hotel owners Stuart and Susannah Macpherson.

On learning Garry is a traditionalist who makes his own breads, pastries and desserts, I silently wished I'd worn an outfit with a little more Lycra in the waistband.

The selection of eleven starters all sounded lovely, with several unusual dishes such as hickory-smoked rabbit saddle and Highland seafood consomme. Being a cheese devotee, I opted for the old-style fried bread fondue, which clearly wasn't the slimmer's special of the day but sounded too good to resist. Mrs satnav plumped for the Finnan haddock, leek and potato risotto tart.

I wasn't sure what to expect of the fondue, and what I was presented with certainly surprised me – a big bowl with large wedges of slow-roasted crispy bread sitting in a sea of strong Scottish cheese and spring onion sauce laced with garlic and white wine. The fondue sauce was fantastic, rich and creamy with just enough wine and garlic to lift it out of the ordinary and into the extraordinary.

Across the table, my sister-in-law was equally happy with her choice. Made with west-coast haddock and laced with leek and potato topped with shavings of Parmesan cheese and basil purée, it had a delicate, sweet and tangy flavour which lingered pleasantly in the mouth.

The hotel has an extensive wine list, and for those not driving or who like to indulge, there's plenty to keep you happy. As I don't possess any great wine-tasting skills, I settled for a rather lovely glass of house red, Merlot, which hit the spot nicely.

For mains, I ordered slow roast shank of lamb and my dinner guest chose baked fillet of salmon. Both were beautifully presented in a way that was stylish without being twee.

Lamb shank is an old, traditional dish and I usually hate it when chefs insist on giving it a makeover. There's always the exception to the rule, and Garry's dish is it. Instead of being served with traditional veg, it came with a flavour-packed boursin, chive and onion potato cake, puy lentils, garlic sausage, a black olive tapenade and mint hollandaise.

It may sound like an odd combination of ingredients, but it worked beautifully. I don't know when I last enjoyed a meat dish that was sexy without being sexed-up.

The salmon was also a fusion of old and new as it came with a vegetable, potato and brie frittata, with sautéed French beans flavoured with bacon and garlic butter, a mild spiced lemon barley kooba and tomato confit cappuccino. It's not often salmon excites us, but this dish looked so good it had us talking long into the night.

While head chef Garry was working at the Atlantic Hotel in Guernsey, he achieved the honour of making the hotel the first to win restaurant of the year three years running; earned two coveted rosette awards from the AA, and became listed in the Michelin restaurant guide.

Owners Stuart and Susannah, a lovely couple who happily chat to all, are confident it will not be long before more honours are bestowed upon him while he is at **Coul House Hotel**.

If his dishes continue to be innovative and of such a high standard, he should have no problem.

Despite his obvious talent, we decided to pass on the desserts and have coffee and a shared cheese board instead. Smooth, rich coffee and a lovely selection of local hard and soft cheeses, served with biscuits, apple, celery and, rather unusually, pickled walnuts, rounded off the meal nicely.

As the sun set slowly in the west, the dining-room was bathed in glorious colours, and as we relaxed over coffee, we chatted about who the people depicted in a large painting of the hotel hanging over the fireplace could be.

It proved to be a painting commemorating an 1888 visit to the hotel, then a mansion built for Sir George Mackenzie, by none other than Queen Victoria.

I wonder if they will commission one to mark the visit of the *Press and Journal* restaurant spies. Now wouldn't that be exciting?

Quality of Food	5
Menu Choice	5
Surroundings	5
Location	4
Service	5
Value for Money	5
Total [out of 30]	**29**

Creelers of Skye and Gumbo Shack

Broadford, Skye

telephone: 01471 822281   website: www.skye-seafood-restaurant.co.uk

"Reach for Skye"

They are a rather friendly lot at the **Creelers of Skye and Gumbo Shack** restaurant at Broadford.

Not only does the grey-haired American waiter love to chat, but so do the chefs – David Wilson and partner Ann Doyle – when they dispense their cuisine from the kitchen.

The approach is certainly different, but then this is an unconventional eatery. While offering up an amazing array of local seafood, it also does a rather tasty line in cajun grub – hence the gumbo – that could rival any eatery in America's Deep South.

Even more unconventional is that the Perth-born chef is a doctor and qualified osteopath. Having burned himself out pursuing a career in London's Harley Street, he decided that the best prescription aged forty was for a new life in Skye pursuing his other passion in life, cooking, a skill he apparently learned as a youngster out of necessity.

The location for his restaurant could not be more apt as **Creelers** is housed in a former butcher's shop – the home of bovine osteopaths – that still retains its meat hooks above the windows and the main fridge in the dining area.

I stopped by for lunch on my way back to the mainland. It was busy, with a steady stream of people taking advantage of the opening hours that see delicious food served from noon until late. I'm glad I was there for lunch, as the evening was fully booked already.

The friendly American waiter – he came from western Michigan but had fallen in love with Skye – took me through the menu and the specials. That the menu came

with photographs proved a hoot as it brought back memories of an evening the year before when I was in a restaurant in Japan where no one spoke English and I selected a steak from among the photos. The steak was wonderful, but then it should have been. It had come straight from Kobe, where they massage their cattle and feed them rice straw and beer.

I was delighted the Skye menu was in English as opposed to Gaelic and that prices were in sterling rather than yen.

There was a decided seafood slant, with king, queen and princess scallops, fish soup, halibut, monkfish, squat lobsters, prawns, Loch Eishort mussels, smoked salmon, conventional salmon, sea bass and haddock as well as cajun haddock.

The gumbo seafood cajun stew came with a health warning that it was particularly hot. I had to agree after having a sample.

Meat lovers could have had French lamb stew, sirloin steak, Italian sausage with penne pasta or chicken gumbo. Instead, I went for the local Loch Eishort mussels as a starter. They proved plump and juicy. Perfectly accompanying them was a delicious white wine and garlic sauce.

My main dish was a fish that I had not knowingly had before – sea bream. It was sautéed in a light wine crème and came with peppercorns served on a bed of wild and basmati rice with some salad.

The bream was cooked to perfection. It was a chunky white fish and rather appealing. It is certainly a fish that I will look out for in future, as it made a difference from my normal choices of either monkfish or haddock.

Desserts were passed over and instead I had the cheese and biscuits. Amazingly, the cheese came with a large helping of biscuits.

I washed down lunch with a bottle of beer and sparkling water.

Dr Wilson proudly boasts on the website: "The restaurant is intended to be as relaxed and informal as possible. Food and wine snobbery is definitely not encouraged. Eating and drinking with one's friends or family is one of life's great pleasures and chef likes nothing better than to hear abundant laughter from the front house while labouring over your main course."

Hear, hear. Laughter is most definitely nature's best medicine.

Quality of Food	5
Menu Choice	5
Surroundings	4
Location	4
Service	5
Value for Money	4
Total *[out of 30]*	**27**

Drumossie Hotel

Old Perth Road, Inverness

telephone: 01463 236451   website: www.drumossiehotel.co.uk

"Upgraded hotel now a class act"

The last time I visited **Drumossie Hotel**, on the outskirts of Inverness, my bridesmaid was convinced the crunchy raw onion she was eating was the most delicious apple grown on Earth since the Garden of Eden was in business. My husband, when not acting out his fantasy of riding home the Grand National winner, thought this highly amusing.

We weren't the only ones acting strangely that night – one chap had earlier declared undying love for a floor mop.

I should explain that all were under the influence of a well known hypnotist of the day. Back then, hypnotists and cabaret shows featured regularly on the **Drumossie's** entertainment programme, and at the time, the hotel was regarded as a cheery, rather than upmarket, venue.

Since then, the hotel and I have changed. I divorced the wannabe jockey and the hotel was granted a divorce from its old image after undergoing an extensive refurbishment.

The hypnotic connection still remains though, as it is very easy to fall under the spell of this new-look hotel, which is now a deluxe four-star establishment. Tastefully upgraded and with an excellent reputation, it is very much the sort of place anyone in the know wants to book for a conference, banquet or wedding.

The hotel, which sits on Old Perth Road, still bears traces of the original 1930s Art Deco architecture and has a lovely marble-floored reception area. It was from here that a friendly receptionist suggested we take a seat in the large lounge which adjoins the area.

The lounge feels like a private club, and there's a real sense of old-fashioned elegance and style which sits well with the general look of the hotel. A mixture of comfy soft leather and jacquard sofas, armchairs, coffee tables and lamps made it the perfect place for us to relax.

Almost immediately, a smartly dressed waiter arrived to whisk away our coats, take a drinks order, deliver complimentary canapés and present the menu, which stated that a team of chefs, under the watchful eye of executive chef Lynsey Horne, would be preparing dishes using fresh, regional and seasonal products.

The two AA Rosette restaurant offers an à la carte menu or a two or three-course set dinner.

We opted for the set three-course menu, which had a choice of five starters, five main dishes and five sweets. But I was immediately faced with a dilemma. I'd noticed an old favourite, beef bourguignon, on the à la carte menu and couldn't resist it. The waiter assured me that picking from both menus wasn't a problem.

When our meal was ready, the

waiter deftly led us to the restaurant while balancing our drinks aloft on a tray on one hand – the other was tucked smartly into the small of his back. A nice touch rarely seen these days. The restaurant was nicely lit with a mixture of soft lighting and candles, while the polished tables were dressed with sparkling glasses and thick linen napkins.

To begin, we tucked into freshly baked bread and creamy butter – a refreshing change from the oil and vinegar that's de rigueur at the moment, along with a complimentary prawn and melon starter. Delicious and unexpected.

My starter of pan-seared Isle of Skye scallops, black pudding, mini potato scones and pea puree looked beautiful and tasted as good as it looked. The freshness of the juicy scallops teamed with the moist pudding made for a winning combination.

My guest's tian of white crab meat and hot smoked salmon topped with caviar crème fraîche with a lime dressing looked equally ravishing – and, I'm told, was light but flavour-packed at the same time. For mains, she had roast loin of lamb served with dauphinoise potato (my favourite), baby spinach parsnip purée and a port and red wine reduction. I was having the aforementioned bourguignon, which came with creamy mashed potatoes.

My gravy had a slightly caramelised tang and was packed with flavours of red wine, garlic, tomato and shallots. While the beef was a tad overdone for my liking, I think it's safe to say this was the best gravy I've tasted in a long time.

The lamb ticked all the right boxes, too. Cooked to pink perfection, it had a sweet and subtle flavour. In terms of looks and taste, her creamy dauphinoise potatoes rivalled the ones I make at home. After sneaking a taste, I'd say they might even be better, darn it.

To finish, I had a delicious Tia Maria and dark chocolate torte with pomegranate syrup and candied kumquats. The richness of the chocolate and the slight tartness of the fruits sent my taste buds into overdrive – something of a regular occurrence here.

My friend finished with a cheese board which had a nice selection of local cheese, celery, savoury biscuits and a small pot of quince paste which looked rather like leftover gravy but added a nice zinginess to proceedings.

Quality of Food	4
Menu Choice	5
Surroundings	5
Location	4
Service	5
Value for Money	4
Total [out of 30]	**27**

Duisdale House Hotel

Isle Ornsay, Sleat, Skye

telephone: 01471 833202   website: www.duisdale.com

"Perfect for a quiet lunch"

The **Duisdale Country House**, from the outside, gives the appearance of a rather Victorian stately home.

Step inside, however, and you will find it has undergone a rather chic – and, by the look of it, expensive – transformation.

Trendy it may be, but it lacked a certain accessory the day I visited – a calling bell. The place was deserted and, with no staff calling button at the reception, I wandered into the bar, the lounge, the dining-room and then into a corridor near the reception before I eventually found a member of the front-of-house team

who confirmed, yes, they did do lunch.

The poor chap was all on his own that lunchtime and I proved the only diner until a couple and their two infant children appeared.

The hotel was deserted, a stark contrast to the evening before when I passed and saw the car park full to overflowing. Skye folk obviously don't do lunch in the way that their urban cousins on the mainland do.

The welcome from the suited staff member was warm and he instantly apologised in the most glorious of west coast accents. Yes, they did lunch, and would I like a seat in the dining-room, he asked.

I was shown to a seat in the conservatory which had magnificent views to the mainland and into the hotel's garden. He was very chatty and told me all about the local attractions and must-visit tourist spots as lunch progressed.

The lunch menu proved a grand affair and not at all what I expected. Mussels, peppered smoked mackerel and Cullen skink were among the starters, while mains included haggis, neeps and tatties, seafood pie, baked mushroom and onion quiche and roast free-range chicken.

I had to sit back in amazement and ordered a glass of Sauvignon, a deliciously fruity number, as I contemplated.

My starter of fresh Loch Eishort mussels cooked in garlic and white wine and served with parsley and a saffron aioli – a sauce made with garlic and olive oil – was exceptional. The aioli, something new for me, certainly added to the taste. The mussels were large, plump and juicy.

I almost decided on venison casserole for a main, but too many bad experiences with this meat resulted in me opting instead for the seafood pie. Venison, when done well, is wonderful, but when bad, is akin to eating a rubber tyre.

The pie, however, hit all the right spots. It was piping hot and came with salmon, squat lobsters and sea bass served in a creamed fish and fine herb velouté with grilled cheese mash.

Delicious was an understatement. The seafood maintained its taste and each bit still retained a bite, signalling it was cooked to perfection.

I should have passed on dessert. Greed, however, got the better of me and soon I was tucking into a wonderful cinnamon spiced apple crumble with bramble parfait and crème anglaise. It was the lesser of the evils that also included home-grown rhubarb crème brûlée, warm chocolate fondant and vanilla cream, a shortcake of Highland berries, mixed berry and almond parfait with honey cream as well as strawberry mousse and **Duisdale** sticky toffee pudding.

A pot of tea followed in the lounge, where the chic new design is very apparent. The dark browns and tans are certainly trendy, but I thought they made the room feel dark. The redeeming feature was, however, the fireplace and the roaring fire.

All in all a very pleasant dining experience which made a great start to 2009.

Quality of Food	5
Menu Choice	5
Surroundings	4
Location	4
Service	3
Value for Money	4
Total [out of 30]	**25**

153

Forss House Hotel

Forss, near Thurso

telephone: 01847 861201   website: www.forsshousehotel.co.uk

"Forss to be reckoned with"

There are few folk who could tell a portly customer that it's too late to worry about having slim-line tonic in your gin.

The cheery Anne, the wafer-thin mine host at the **Forss House Hotel** at Forss, near Thurso, can.

The glint in her eye and the cheerful nature in which she made the remark after I ordered my gin and slim-line made my night.

But then that's Anne, a full-blown Highlander who later showed an amazing knowledge of the more than 300 different whiskies that adorn the hotel bar. She also had the perfect way of taking the fire out of some of Scotland's more peaty malts: a 'teardrop' of water from the brass tap that sits atop the bar.

The gin was just what I needed after a tortuous journey north on the dreaded A9 from Inverness. Two rather large loads kept traffic at a snail's pace for what seemed like hours, although in reality only from Tain to Golspie.

My gin was the perfect accompaniment as I chilled and studied the menu. Would it be rabbit, smoked salmon, pigeon or Sinclair Bay crab for starters? Or what about the celeriac soup with smoked eel and white truffle?

I'm not courageous enough to have rabbit or pigeon; not nearly adventurous, I hear you say? Well, I have had smoked eel before and, as they say, once was more than enough.

Smoked salmon seemed the safest option for me, although there was none left by the time I ordered, so I went with the gravalax alternative. Meaty and chunky it might have been, but oh so tender and melt-in-the-mouth. It was served with a wonderfully tangy sauce.

I was mightily impressed with the main courses, all of which were distinctly local and just how they should be. The Mey Selections beef, the Lairg roe deer, freshly caught hake or Watten pork?

The last sent my curiosity into overdrive. Pork from Watten, west o' Wick?

Absolutely. Farmers Kenny and Isobel Campbell keep their own pigs at Watten.

Given that most supermarket pork these days is white and tasteless, this home-grown product was crying out to be consumed.

I'm glad it didn't let me down, either. Tasty and succulent it was, and just like old-fashioned pork in days of yore when pigs were fed proper diets rather than the soya, grain and fishmeal which their stomachs are pumped full of these days. Little wonder supermarket pork has no taste.

I'll also say they know how to cook vegetables at the **Forss House**. The broccoli that came with my pork was done to perfection, retaining a delicious bite.

It proved an interesting evening as Anne and her assistants scurried around the packed dining-room attending to the needs of everyone Three Dutchmen, who had earlier been stalking deer, had a little difficulty with English. They found a sympathetic ear in Anne who was able to advise on their dinner and tell them in wonderfully descriptive terms about the hake.

The desserts were, sadly, all too sweet for me, so I passed on the glazed chocolate brownie with cranberry sauce, the Forss summer pudding with yoghurt foam and fresh nutmeg, prune, apple and butterscotch compote and the Halkirk raspberry tart with crème fraîche ice cream and, instead, opted for the biscuits and cheese complete with a glass of vintage port.

The cheese selection was good but, as ever, there were not nearly enough biscuits to accompany it. Is there a biscuit shortage in Scotland's restaurants?

The **Forss House** proved a wonderful venue and the food exceptionally good, although the dining-room on a dark, autumnal night proved a little gloomy. More light may be needed, or candles. The hotel is also not the easiest to find on a dark night and better signposting would help.

Quality of Food	5
Menu Choice	5
Surroundings	4
Location	3
Service	5
Value for Money	4
Total [out of 30]	**26**

Lovat Arms Hotel
Loch Ness, Fort Augustus

telephone: 01456 459250   website: www.lovatarms-hotel.com

"Lovat – just love it"

I would like readers to think it's my fabulous investigative skills which allow me to reveal the following about the **Lovat Arms Hotel**, Fort Augustus.

Last month was a hectic time, what with a wedding, an eightieth birthday celebration and a fundraising *Playboy*-themed

party taking place. Keen to know the secrets of head chef Jim Murphy's delicious baked fillet of Lochaber salmon and cassoulet? I can reveal that, too.

By now, you may be thinking one of two things: this restaurant spy is really good or – and this is far more likely – the spy has logged on to the hotel's website.

These days, any restaurant worth its low-sodium salt has a website allowing potential diners the opportunity to give the menus the once over.

Two items made the **Lovat's** website better than most. First, it included a 'blog' – a chatty news page revealing, in a homely style, details of recent and forthcoming events at the hotel. Secondly, and very unusually, it had a page of downloadable recipes for a two-course dinner party for four people.

In a world where hi-tech, instant information is king, it's a brilliant idea and certainly helped persuade my little party of three that it would be worth making the trip along the beautiful, but rather twisty, road from Inverness to Fort Augustus.

While the website may be uber-modern, I was delighted to find that the family-run Victorian hotel is not and retains much of its original charm and character.

The first recorded date of the **Lovat Arms** being a hotel is thought to have been in 1869. Since then, it has provided hospitality for generations of visitors and locals alike and witnessed lots of change. The most recent took place earlier this year when Caroline Gregory, manager of the hotel and daughter of owners David and Geraldine, oversaw a total refurbishment which introduced hi-tech and chic style but kept lots of the old-world charm.

We opted for the promotional Dine Around menu, which offers three courses. As the hotel has just received its first AA rosette, it seemed good value for money.

When our meal was ready, we were shown into the formal dining-room, a charming traditional room simply decorated and furnished with objets d'art and a lovely grand piano topped with framed family photographs.

As we tucked into a selection of warm rolls, our starters arrived. Two of us plumped for the smoked Lochaber salmon served atop a warm blini with crème fraîche, lemon and a caper and endive salad, while the younger member had the spring roll stuffed with shredded duck and bean sprout served with a hoi sin dressing.

The salmon, lots of generously cut slices with a strong, almost peat-smoke, flavour, was superb and went beautifully with the crisp salad.

Spring rolls can be dull as dishwater, but this new version of an old Oriental favourite was highly praised, both for the lightness of the batter and the sweet, tenderness of the duck. For mains, I ordered the fillet of pork, my partner requested stuffed chicken and my son the best end of Highland lamb.

The sweet smell of the roasted lamb wafted across the dining-room, whetting our appetites and making me wish I'd ordered this dish instead.

Thankfully, our family policy of always trying a little of each other's dishes meant I did get a wee taster.

The lamb, tender and beautifully pink on the inside, was served with clapshot, Lochaber haggis, roast cherry tomatoes and a rosemary and malt whisky jus. A feast for the eyes and taste buds alike, it looked every inch an award-winner.

My partner's roast chicken, stuffed with spinach, garlic and Parmesan cheese and accompanied by champ potato, peppered leeks and sweet pea purée, was also declared a winner – although the purée was rather like posh mushy peas. My pan-roasted fillet of pork came with braised Savoy cabbage, pancetta, herb-roasted potatoes and a flavoursome Madeira jus. It's a long time since I've seen cabbage on a menu, possibly because it's not the sexiest veg on the block, but its absence made its return all the more welcome.

My pork was slightly dry – more to do with my preferences than the chef's skills – and I could have done with a splash more gravy, but that aside, it was very good, especially when washed down with a warm glass of Shiraz.

From the sweet menu, I was tempted by the sound of the sticky toffee pudding served with cream and a rum and vanilla toffee sauce. The pud was as light as a feather and there was just enough rum in the sauce to raise it to the next level. The contented sighs coming from my companions let me know the caramelised lemon cream tart, served with raspberry water ice and berry coulis, and the chef's extra creamy cheesecake were hitting the spot, too.

Quality of Food	5
Menu Choice	4
Surroundings	4
Location	5
Service	5
Value for Money	4
Total *[out of 30]*	**27**

No 1 Bistro at Mackay's Hotel

Ebenezer Street, Wick

telephone: 01955 602323   website: www.mackayshotel.co.uk

"And at No 1 . . ."

Ever gone to a restaurant and forgotten your reading glasses? Dashed annoying, is it not? Your arms never seem long enough to get the type on the menu in focus.

Wick's **No 1 Bistro** at Mackay's Hotel has the solution, though. As well as dishing up some rather fine grub, it also sells those magnifying glasses that are the saviour of any absent-minded spectacle wearer.

The spectacles – for the more fashion-conscious, it has to be said, and considerably more expensive than the £2 versions from a high-street chemist – are housed in one of two impressive displays

at the bistro, whose entrance is on Ebenezer Street, the world's smallest street at only 6ft 9in.

The other display at **No 1** confirms the hotel's proud record of serving up local produce. It shows pictures of the champion cattle and prime sheep that it has bought at the nearby Caithness Livestock Centre, at Quoybrae, run by Aberdeen and Northern Marts.

It is a great shame that many other establishments do not follow the lead of hotel owner Murray Lamont in supporting local farmers by buying direct from them and paying a premium price.

Having had to make do with a

sandwich for lunch as they had run out of mince in Kirkwall – yes, no mince in Orkney, where the cattle population outnumbers humans by three to one – I was somewhat hungry.

No 1's menu certainly made me salivate. It was filled with delicious local produce, including Wick haggis and potato scone, Highland venison, Caithness beef and sea bass and Scrabster haddock.

That said, there were also Scottish free-range chicken, Scottish salmon, hot smoked mackerel and Caithness lamb sausages.

There was just one item on the bill of fare that I turned my nose up at – goat's cheese soufflé. I have yet to appreciate goat's cheese as a food source. Goats smell awful, and so does their cheese, which tastes equally bad as the whiff they give off.

No 1's staff are young, but they were as keen as mustard to secure my order.

I was taken in by the blurb and opted for the Cullen Skink, for which **No 1** says on the menu it has an enviable reputation. Main course was a 10oz sirloin steak sourced from those wonderful people at Mey Selections who have done so much – with a little help from the Prince of Wales – in boosting the fortunes of livestock producers in the far north.

There were only two words

to describe the soup – absolutely divine.

I had thought an old contact, Norrie Grierson, who used to be mine host at the Pennan Inn, in picturesque Pennan, was the bee's knees when it came to Cullen Skink. But Mr Lamont and his team beat even Norrie.

Their soup was wonderfully creamy and came with chunky potatoes and what seemed like an entire smoked haddock. I could have gorged myself on it for the rest of the evening, but resisted the temptation.

The steak was wonderful, and oh so tasty.

The home-made chips it was served with were excellent although, if nitpicking, the broccoli and carrot batons were slightly cold.

The local theme continued into the desserts, with Halkirk strawberries on offer and home-made ice cream. For the more adventurous, there was watermelon and blackberry jelly with home-made rasp sorbet or a dark chocolate cake with blueberry ice cream.

I opted for the Highland cheeses, a selection that came from Orkney, I discovered, after sending the waitress back to the kitchen to find out their provenance.

The cheeses were served with home-made chutney and oatcakes, although my ever-persistent bugbear was that the biscuits appeared to be rationed.

No 1 was extremely busy on the night that I visited, but that did not faze the youthful staff. Mr Lamont also visited every table and spoke to the diners, which was good to see.

My only issue was over the wine. I wanted a bottle of Chardonnay, but the barman shook his head on being told of my request by the waitress. She came back not with the wine list to make another choice, but said I couldn't get that and instead pointed me to the laminated wine list on the table.

It offered only glasses of wine, so it was a case of ordering one with the soup and then selecting a rather fruity Echo Point Shiraz from Australia's Limestone coast

to accompany my steak.

All in all, it was a very pleasant meal in wonderful surroundings that really hammered home that this was an eatery proud to serve local produce. If only others would follow **No 1's** example we would have two of Scotland's prime rural industries – agriculture and fisheries – rejoicing.

Here's hoping **No 1's** enthusiasm proves highly infectious across the rest of Scotland and that those who source from catering giants see the error of their ways.

Quality of Food	5
Menu Choice	5
Surroundings	5
Location	4
Service	4
Value for Money	5
Total *[out of 30]*	**28**

Rocpool Reserve

Culduthel Road, Inverness

telephone: 01463 240089   website: www.rocpool.com

"Recommended – unreservedly"

I was admiring the hills which stretched out before me into the distance above Loch Ness and longed to stride out in exploration of the treasures which lay beyond.

What a fine day for a walk in the hills.

But enough of that, I thought, as I glanced away from the view through the window, snuggled deeper in my comfy, white leather dining chair and took a closer look at the menu.

The only Highland adventure for me that day was to be clambering across the impressive peaks and admiring the mouthwatering views on the menu at **Rocpool Reserve** boutique hotel and restaurant in Inverness.

I guessed we were in for the red-carpet treatment. After all, you cannot miss it – a huge red carpet stretches from the front door and runs majestically through the reception corridor and into the distance.

Red seemed to feature quite strongly in the overall colour scheme. There is even a Red Room for private dining and meetings, but black or creamy white took pride of place on the carpets, the walls and the leather furniture everywhere else. Even the impressive Georgian building which is home to **Rocpool Reserve** has a tasty coating of soft, creamy colours.

This newcomer had won a string of awards already and it had only been open a few months.

One of them, very highly commended among Scotland's sexiest hotels of the year, caught my eye in particular for some reason. As a trained reporter, I felt it my duty to keep my eyes peeled, on your behalf, for any activity under this heading in a tireless quest for the truth, but I have nothing to reveal, so to speak.

The ambience did have a sort of sensual tingle, I have to say, or was that my stomach rumbling?

The establishment's blurb purrs suggestively that it is "cool and clandestine". It also has lashings of elegance and style.

A luxury boutique hotel and restaurant is something new for Inverness and it sits on a hill, not far from Inverness Castle, amid similarly elegant and substantial properties.

Rocpool Reserve is related to Rocpool Rendezvous restaurant, alongside the river in Inverness city centre, which also has a fine reputation.

The main dining-room, with its large window looking out towards the hills, is divided into three comfortable sections, which adds to the intimacy of the occasion. In the middle section, for example, there is a huge internal window on one side, enabling you to see the comings and goings in the main corridor.

While **Rocpool Reserve** is pitched elegantly upmarket, it also keeps the restaurant busy during the day by offering a reasonably priced lunch menu, to run alongside the dinner menu.

As I was visiting at lunchtime with a colleague, important decisions had to be made: could we choose from both?

No problem, we were told. So, not surprisingly, I grabbed the dinner menu while my colleague was left with the cheaper lunch version. As it happened, you could not put a green salad leaf between them in terms of quality.

Our Polish waitress quickly delivered some delicious breads, such as focaccia with olive oil, and our selections were under way.

For starters, I chose carpaccio of Aberdeen-Angus beef, cooked medium rare and cut thinly into medallion shapes, with rucola salad leaves dressed in virgin oil and aged balsamic vinegar.

My colleague went for salad of smoked, peppered duck with roasted beetroot and honey-mustard dressing.

Both were beautifully presented with good taste combinations and, although they sounded fairly substantial, they were actually pleasingly light.

For mains, my choice was grilled fillet of wild sea bass on asparagus, with a ravioli of crab and lobster and vanilla foam.

On the other side of the table was braised lamb shoulder with roasted pumpkin, olive-oil mash and rosemary gravy.

My fish dish was an impressive sight and swimming in striking contrasts. The fish was deliciously light and moist, while the ravioli berthed alongside was a delightful taste contrast. It was an excellent dish.

Contrasts and rich combinations were also unfolding with the lamb dish opposite and its unusual supporting cast of pumpkin and olive-oil mash – a great hit with my colleague.

We rounded off with red fruit jelly and ice cream, and mille-feuille poached pear. We felt as though we had enjoyed quite a gastronomic roller-coaster, but left pleasantly satisfied rather than over-full.

There were neat touches along the way, as well. At one point, I went off to investigate the rather cool cocktail bar with its chandeliers and lime-coloured, back-lit bar counters and left my napkin sprawled on the table. On my return, one of the waitresses had folded the napkin neatly and put it back on my seat.

I had been staring at an eye-catching table decoration in the hall – a large, unusually shaped glass object full of apples.

"Are those real?" I asked a passing female member of staff, not wanting to look an idiot by picking up what might be an extravagant work of art.

"Of course they are," she laughed, slightly nervously.

I had been under **Rocpool Reserve's** spell for too long. It was time to go or I would have quite happily stayed all afternoon.

Quality of Food	5
Menu Choice	5
Surroundings	5
Location	4
Service	5
Value for Money	4
Total *[out of 30]*	**28**

News from Rocpool : *Albert Roux OBE and Maître Cuisinier de France is to open his first restaurant in Scotland. The multi-award winning chef, often cited as the most influential of his profession, has announced his plans to take over the kitchens of* **Rocpool Reserve***, Inverness. His restaurant,* **Chez Roux***, opens on 1 April 2009.*

The Crannoch Hotel

Blantyre Street, Cullen

telephone: 01542 840210   website: www.crannoch.hotel.btinternet.co.uk

"Simply delicious"

There's something extra special about good country cooking.

The simplicity of it means that you get exactly what it says on the menu without wondering what on earth a jus is, or a red-wine reduction.

As increasing numbers of restaurants and chefs bamboozle the public at large with their technical terms to make their menus look more impressive than they really are, there will always be a place for good simple fare – for me, at least. I've thrived on it for nearly forty years.

The **Crannoch Hotel**, at Cullen, is an excellent example of an eatery that doesn't appear to pander to the latest foodie trends and words.

Tucked away on Blantyre Street, behind Cullen's impressive Square, the **Crannoch**, from the outside, doesn't really jump out and hit you as a groovy place to go.

Stepping inside, you are also left questioning whether you've made the right decision as the vestibule is rather drab.

Walk through the restaurant door, though, and you see the first signs of something different – very different.

Striking black and white walls, minimalist furnishings, strange desk-like tables, trendy chairs, ultra-modern lights and a highly polished floor leave you doing a double-take. Is this really Cullen?

We went on Sunday for Mother's Day, when we discovered we weren't the only ones who had ventured to the **Crannoch**. The restaurant was packed – a sure sign of its popularity.

There was a special set three-course menu. Some might say restrictive, but I thought it wonderful as it made the selection so much easier.

Mother went for the melon pearls and fruit sorbet, while father and I ordered the cajun spiced mushrooms with a garlic mayonnaise for starters.

Our mushrooms were not for the faint-hearted, both in terms of their spicy heat and the exceptionally large portion size. Mother was more than happy with her selection, although she did initially question how she would be able to get to the melon given the amount of sorbet that had been placed on top of the fruit pearls.

We were adventurous with the main courses – each choosing something different. I went for the turkey with all the trimmings, mother the roast silverside and father – somewhat unusually – the vegetarian option, cheese savoury

baskets with a vegetable stroganoff and seasonal salad.

We thought the starters were big, but that was nothing compared with the mains as they were truly man-size portions.

The beef was exceptionally good and melt-in-the-mouth, but a slice was left on the plate because of the quantity. The turkey was wonderfully cooked and moist. He who ordered veggie was impressed.

The mains came served with plates of boiled and roast potatoes, brussels sprouts and mashed neeps.

Many decry the smallest of the brassicas. I, however, adore them and firmly believe they are much underrated. Yes, they are horrible if they are overcooked. Get them right, though, and they are wonderful.

The **Crannoch** had them to perfection, although I would personally take issue with them for scoring the bottom of the sprouts.

Desserts were again simple – a raspberry and hazelnut roulade with vanilla ice cream and fresh cream; brandy baskets filled with fruits of the forest ice cream laced with a sweet strawberry coulis and drizzled with cream.

Mother went for the former. Father and I just wanted ice cream.

Cullen is famous for its ice cream, but the **Crannoch's** certainly did not appear to come from the wonderful ice-cream shop just off The Square. We nonetheless enjoyed what came our way.

We left impressed, if somewhat full. The young waiting staff were attentive and smartly attired, although a little shy and quiet.

Quality of Food	5
Menu Choice	5
Surroundings	4
Location	4
Service	3
Value for Money	5
Total [out of 30]	**26**

Sands Hotel

Burray, Orkney

telephone: 01856 731298   website: www.thesandshotel.co.uk

"Orkney eatery a delight"

The wealth of good eateries in Orkney never ceases to amaze me. On all my visits northwards, I have never been disappointed with the standard of food or the service.

We had crossed an unusually calm Pentland Firth on the 'short crossing' from Gills Bay to St Margaret's Hope.

Normally, I would have ventured from Scrabster and headed to Stromness. But a faster crossing was needed on this occasion as both of my passengers are landlubbers who tend to get ill bobbing up and down in a boat.

My other main reason for usually going with NorthLink is the dashed fine food you get on board. That cannot be said for the Pentland Ferries' vessel, as a waft of fat and chips greeted us as we climbed up the stairs from the car deck.

Still, what proved to be an income loser for Pentland Ferries gave us a reason to find a local hostelry as soon as we landed for something to eat, especially as it was nearing 8.30pm.

The first port of call was **Sands Hotel**, just off the road from St Margaret's Hope to Kirkwall, our ultimate destination.

This hotel, down by the pier at Burray, has recently been

refurbished. It was busy that Friday night, in fact very busy, but still a place was found for the three of us in the conservatory. The hotel owner is obviously something of a green-fingered expert, judging by the various pot plants around and above us.

The welcome was warm and the menus presented. She who prefers the soil to the water was immediately taken with the scallops, both as a starter in the form of scallops with a citrus sauce and served on a garlic mash and as a main in scallops on a bed of leek and bacon with an orange butter sauce.

Sadly for mother, the scallops were off as poor weather in the previous two days had prevented the fishermen getting out and the ferries from landing.

Father and I decided on the fish soup served with a beremeal bannock, while she who must be obeyed opted for the deep-fried Orkney cheese, from Grimbister, with the addition of a spot of cranberry.

Our soup was deliciously creamy with some welcome chunky additions. Mother was suitably impressed with her cheese, too.

The main course, for me, was simple. I just couldn't be this far north in Scotland without sampling Orkney's finest – its beef. A medium-rare sirloin steak it had to be, served with vine tomatoes,

mushrooms, broccoli and potatoes.

I was not disappointed. It was cooked to perfection, wonderfully tender and oh so tasty. Little wonder that, the following day, we left the island with a box of various cuts from the Dounby Butcher, whose tender and tasty beef we immediately fell in love with after sampling it at Taste of Grampian in Inverurie in June.

Mother decided on halibut, the catch of the day. It came with a Cointreau sauce and a number of blueberries around the plate to give the dish some added colour.

The halibut was perfectly cooked, but the sauce seemed somewhat lacking in Cointreau, although her taste buds may have been neutralised somewhat by the large gin before the meal.

Father is the fisher, although that activity is most definitely restricted to riverbanks rather than the sea as he, too, is among the world's worst sailors.

He decided on the salmon, although in Orkney that is of the farmed variety rather than the river-caught type he prefers.

The salmon came herb-crusted with a sprig of rosemary and a lemon and caper sauce, which in itself proved mighty fine, as I sneaked a taste.

A welcome addition to the main course were the plates of vegetables and potatoes. No soggy veg either, but wonderfully crisp and with a bit of bite – just as they should be.

The two elders did not want dessert, which came in the form of sticky toffee pudding, white chocolate panacotta, clootie dumpling, home-made Orkney fudge cheesecake, coffee and walnut parfait, Orkney ice cream or the raspberry cranachan bombe which I decided to sample.

It was a masterpiece with what could only be described as a raspberry sorbet on the outside surrounding a whipped cream and oatmeal centre.

Not your usual cranachan, it has to be said, but then, when it comes to food, Orkney is no ordinary place.

Good food abounds, so get north and sample it.

We were in the conservatory and it did feel, once other guests had gone, that we had been forgotten about, although the banter from the staff more than made up for that.

One of Orkney's great delights is its cheese, but there was no cheeseboard, nor biscuits and cheese, on the menu the night we called. Better signposting for we sooth-moothers in Orkney would also have been a help.

Quality of Food	5
Menu Choice	4
Surroundings	5
Location	4
Service	4
Value for Money	5
Total *[out of 30]*	**27**

63 Tay Street Restaurant

63 Tay Street, Perth

telephone: 01738 441451   website: www.63taystreet.com

"Dining as it should be"

The poet William McGonagall, the man who made an art form of bad verse, once wrote:

> *Beautiful silvery Tay,*
> *With your landscapes,*
> *so lovely and gay,*
> *Along each side of your waters,*
> *to Perth all the way.*

All the way and past the front door of **63 Tay Street**, the restaurant of husband and wife team Jeremy and Shona Wares.

Seated at a table by the window, we watched daylight fade to dusk over the river, its fast-flowing waters swollen by the precipitation from the last blast of winter.

That it was unseasonably chilly for April did not matter. The atmosphere was as cosy as the temperature, as the intimate dining room quickly filled to capacity. It became clear why we had had to make a reservation weeks in advance.

Menus in hand, we nibbled on the delicate hors d'oeuvres, Parmesan biscuits and light, cheese-filled pastries.

The food choice is kept to a minimum, and diners can choose from a two, three or even four-course option. There are set prices for each, although some choices carry a supplement. With the various permutations, there was more than enough to keep us busy for several minutes.

The extensive wine list also requires more than a cursory glance, although our eventual selection came from the opening pages, one of **63 Tay Street's** house whites. The 2004 Picpoul de Pinet was delicate and refreshing and an absolute bargain. All that was required was a warm summer's evening in the Languedoc to make the wine-drinking experience complete.

To partner it, my wife opted to start with crab mayonnaise with avocado fritter and a crab vinaigrette, while I chose the crispy duck leg confit with a sweet chilli accompaniment.

The dishes arrived on elegant monogrammed plates, and the presentation could not be faulted. Thankfully, neither could the quality of the cooking or the taste. Both were first-class. The crab was light and refreshing, while the duck skin had a delicate crunch and the meat fell from the bone.

We had skipped course two, which had a choice of soup, oysters or sorbet in favour of the main event.

My selection, roasted fillet of beef with a parsnip and sweet potato puree and Savoy cabbage was as fine a piece of meat as I've

eaten on my travels for this journal.

The herb-crusted rack of lamb across the table was not such a big hit. Served with dauphinoise potatoes and Provençal-style vegetables, it gained good marks for taste but was marked down as it took more effort than one would have expected to remove it from the bone.

Undeterred, we moved on to the sweet selection, which was another high spot on an evening already littered with peaks. My wife is not a dessert person, but was persuaded to try the rhubarb crème brûlée with a rhubarb sorbet. Myself, being a traditional sort, could not see past the steamed ginger pudding with crème anglaise and vanilla ice cream.

If you remember rhubarb and custard boiled sweets, and cherish those memories, the first of those would have had you in raptures. Much more delicate on the taste buds, but still with that sweet and slightly sour sensation. The ginger pudding was excellent, not stodgy at all and with just the right level of gingeriness. A food review and a new word!

Keen to enjoy our evening to the last, we ordered two glasses of the Picpoul and sipped as we reached our verdict on **63 Tay Street**.

The walls are adorned with awards of all shapes and sizes, and the broad window ledges scattered with cuisine bibles in which it gets a mention. Jeremy and Shona have built up a good reputation for their business, and deservedly so.

While Mr Wares works his magic in the kitchen, his wife is in command front of house and they make a formidable team. This was dining as it should be – a simple menu, good service and food to match. The view, should you grab a window table, would have won the approval of Mr McGonagall, given his affection for the stretch of water which flows past the front door.

Quality of Food	4
Menu Choice	5
Surroundings	5
Location	5
Service	4
Value for Money	5
Total [out of 30]	**28**

Ardeonaig Hotel and Restaurant

South Road Loch Tay, Ardeonaig, Perthshire

telephone: 01567 820400   website: www.ardeonaighotel.co.uk

"Simply perfect"

It is often said that to survive as a food business in Scotland's rural hinterland you have to be extra special.

South African Pete Gottgens, however, goes one step further with his iconic **Ardeonaig Hotel**, which is tucked away in the middle of nowhere on the southern banks of Loch Tay.

This is as near food paradise and

173

service perfection as you will ever get.

You have to be determined to get to Ardeonaig, though. The ten miles of twisty single-track road from picturesque Kenmore is not for the faint-hearted. That we chose a dark winter's night of rain, sleet and then frost made it an even bigger challenge.

Still, the reward was more than worthwhile – a meal that restored my faith in the ability of chefs to do miracles.

From start to finish this dinner was divine. The service was similarly amazing.

We were greeted with a welcoming handshake from the hostess and served drinks in the bar, where we looked over the set five-course menu. It was then off to the upstairs study rather than the restaurant or the cellar dining-room as there were only six dining that evening.

The waiter and waitresses knew their stuff – and their wines. We had opted for the wine 'flights', and the variation they offered with each course, rather than the conventional bottle. We were not disappointed. The Haute Cabrière Chardonnay-Pinot Noir – South African, naturally, as were all the others – was particularly good.

We started with delicious squid – tentacles and all – served with caper berries and salad leaves. This was followed by very tasty St Monans'

smoked haddock with a quail's egg and mustard sauce.

It was, however, the Ardeonaig's twist on Blackface lamb that proved amazing. The shoulder of lamb, braised for eight hours and served on a bed of sweet potatoes with a Madeira jus, was, in a word – wow.

Who would have ever thought that Blackface lamb could be so tender and oh so tasty? That it could be picked apart with a fork confirmed the much undervalued asset that is grazing Scotland's hills, glens and islands.

It really is a disaster – and embarrassing national disgrace – that other eateries cannot go to similar lengths in creating dishes to bring out the real flavour and texture of the meat from our native hill sheep breed.

What better way of resolving the financial crisis faced by many hill sheep producers – who are putting away sheep in their thousands – than by making Blackface lamb a must-have dish and truly rewarding them for their efforts?

I feel better for that rant. It really upsets me that chefs can be so lazy in some places and, rather than go to the effort of making something special from a local delicacy, can – with considerable professionalism – turn it into inedible, chewy and fatty dross, or simply for convenience, order imported lamb and then pass it off as Scottish as it has been butchered here.

Back to the menu, though, and desserts. Diabetics should not really have such things, but the pair of us simply could not resist the traditional South African Malva pudding – a heavy sponge and not at all dissimilar to the pudding normally served with sticky toffee sauce. No sticky toffee sauce, thankfully, this time. Instead, three rather sweet apricots and ice cream.

We were impressed not just with the food, though, but with the sourcing of it. The lamb came from the neighbouring farm, Braes of Ardeonaig, run by Helen Taylor and her family. High time she and countless others were properly rewarded for their Blackies.

The Ardeonaig's sparkling water is made on the premises and sourced from the nearby Finglen Burn.

Our evening ended in the white room with a refreshing cup of tea.

Before that, however, we were given a tour of the hotel and taken to the various dining-rooms, as well as the kitchen with its fancy electronic sliding door.

I was very impressed after one of the other diners asked for an explanation of what was so special about the Blackface breed. The waitress came back with a leaflet from the Blackface Sheep Breeders' Association extolling its virtues.

If only every other restaurant did the same then them thar hills would be filled with true gold and Scotland's sheep farmers, for once, would be properly rewarded.

Quality of Food	5
Menu Choice	4
Surroundings	4
Location	4
Service	5
Value for Money	5
Total *[out of 30]*	**27**

Ballathie House Hotel
Kinclaven, Stanley, Perthshire

telephone: 01250 883268   website: www.ballathiehousehotel.com

"Getting lost – but on to a winner"

I hold a well known route matching website to blame for my getting lost in deepest Perthshire.

Rather foolishly, I chose to follow it instead of using commonsense and a decent map to find my way to **Ballathie House Hotel** in Kinclaven.

The online version led me up the garden path to Blairgowrie, where I was forced to admit defeat and seek directions from helpful staff at the tourist information centre.

New map in hand, we set off again, and soon found ourselves driving through some of the bonniest tree-lined roads I've seen in a long time. There wasn't a cloud to be seen in the sky, but taking the tourist route to Kinclaven, instead of the suggested busy A9, offered plenty of silver linings.

The feel-good mood continued as we made our way down the long and winding driveway to the picturesque country house hotel, which is just a few miles from the hamlet of Stanley.

Rabbits and squirrels appeared to emerge from nowhere to have a look at us, much to the delight of my youngsters, while I found it hard to keep my eyes on the single-track road as they were hypnotically drawn towards the vivid rhododendrons and lush greenery. So far, so beautiful.

The hotel itself is a wee jewel of a place, set within a stunning 1,500-acre estate through which the sparkling River Tay flows.

Dating back to the 17th century, it was sympathetically converted to a luxury hotel in the early 1970s, but retains all the charm, understated elegance and grandeur of a private country house.

Ranked as one of the top 200 hotels in Britain, it has also picked up a gong or two along the way for its food, which puts a modern spin on traditional Scottish cuisine.

We were eating in the main dining-room, a pretty room with pale yellow panels decorated with exotic birds of paradise and picture windows overlooking the river.

Both the lunch and dinner menus change daily – which is great for residential guests.

On this occasion, there were five starters to choose from. I plumped for the roma tomato gateaux with truffled goat's cheese and a fine herb dressing, while my teenagers both opted for smooth chicken and goose liver parfait served with mini oatcakes and an apple and walnut salad.

My gateaux was actually a tower of fresh peeled plum tomatoes, sun-dried tomatoes and fluffy whisked goat's cheese, which came with a piquant basil dressing. Small but intensely flavoursome, it was a delicious way to start the meal.

Although fond of strong flavours, the parfait was a little too rich and gamey for the teens, who managed to eat only half before admitting defeat. Naturally, they made me sample it to make sure I understood they weren't being overly fussy.

I'd say they were. Yes, it was very strong, but generally anything featuring goose liver is. Being young, they didn't quite appreciate that and made the mistake of thinking it would be more like a Brussels pâté.

But that's how you learn, so there was no nagging from me.

Next up for me was a sweet, creamy bowl of cauliflower and cumin soup, which had a delicious, delicate flavour, while the others tucked into a refreshing glass of mango water ice.

After much dithering and debate about what to have for mains, I settled on roast loin of local venison, my daughter chose the roast guinea fowl and my son stuck with his favourite, carved sirloin of Scotch beef served medium rare.

I can't say who had the better dish as all three were superb. My venison came with potatoes with a hint of almond, braised red cabbage, baby leeks and a classic Madeira sauce.

The venison was so succulent I could have eaten it with a butter knife, while the braised red cabbage added both colour and flavour to the plate.

The roast guinea fowl went down a storm. Served with a black pudding ballotine, pea risotto, sautéed mushrooms and a cider sauce, it had my daughter doing her best to wind up her brother by saying she had made the best choice.

Not quite as gamey as grouse, another of her favourites, but with far more flavour than a chicken, it went really well with the sweet black pudding.

Meanwhile, head chef Andrew Wilkie had succeeded in doing something I regularly fail to do – silencing my son.

Apart from pointing out that his sirloin was exactly the right shade of pink and suggesting the dauphinoise potato was as good as mine, he sat in happy silence, with only the occasional murmur of approval leaving his lips.

By now, dusk was falling and through the windows we could see dainty pipistrelle bats coming to life outside and flying gracefully between the trees.

But before we stepped out for a closer look, there was the dessert menu to tackle. I finished with a cup of coffee and a rather nice selection of French and Scottish cheeses, which came with cold grapes, crisp celery, oatcakes and quince. The teens chose the same sweet – crème brûlée with home-made shortbread.

Currently their favourite choice of sweet – banoffee pie is so last year, apparently – they agreed that this thick, creamy vanilla-scented dish, with its crisp, golden caramelised lid, was among the best they had sampled.

United in their praise for it, they also ganged up on me to demand that I buy a mini blowtorch so they can make crème brûlée at home. I think not.

The hotel has an enviable selection of 350 wines to choose from, with about a dozen available by the glass.

Before driving off into thè sunset, we had a stroll through the tranquil gardens and, right on cue, an owl hooted and a gorgeous white tail baby deer cantered by. Well worth getting lost for, I'd say.

Quality of Food	5
Menu Choice	4
Surroundings	5
Location	4
Service	5
Value for Money	4
Total [out of 30]	**27**

Café Tabou

4 St John's Place, Perth

telephone: 01738 446698   website: www.cafetabou.co.uk

"A taste of Paris in Fair City"

Good French restaurants are hard to come by, unless you happen to be in Paris for the weekend. Even then, you might end up with a distinctly average meal at a price which is likely to elicit a cry of *sacré bleu*, unless a benevolent local has tipped you off in advance.

Perth has little in common with Paris, save they both begin with the same letter and have a river running through the middle. But it does have a very fine restaurant, which would not be out of place on the banks of the Seine rather than the Tay.

The Auld Alliance is alive and well and never more evident than within the walls of **Café Tabou**. I have to confess it had not been our first choice for our evening out, but it came off the substitute's bench and scored the gastronomic equivalent of a hat-trick.

The restaurant is housed in a former glazier's premises. Some might suggest the owners saw a window of opportunity when they spotted its potential as the location for their own little corner of Brittany or Burgundy. I wouldn't dare use such a dreadful pun.

Painted bright red on the outside, the inside is crammed full of bistro-style tables and chairs which tested the art of waiting to the limit. Eric, who spent the evening dishing out food, beverages and advice to us in equal measures, was a fantastic ambassador for both his employer and his native country.

Having found service lacking on our last Egon Ronay-esque venture, Eric's efforts on our latest trip were worthy of a special mention.

On the night in question, we spotted the company transport parked at the kitchen door. It stated that **Café Tabou** served breakfast, lunch and dinner. Later, when scanning the menu, we discovered the venue also dishes up a pre-theatre offering between 5.30 and 7pm. There is clearly never a dull moment at this place.

Our table wasn't ready when we arrived, but Eric whisked us to another which we could use while making our food and wine choices.

An exclusively French selection on the latter might put off some who have been reared on the offerings of the New World, but the alcoholic version of the grape is something of a hobby of mine and I was intrigued by one particular offering.

I narrowed the choice down to two, and sought advice. I was pointed in the direction of the Saumur Champigny red from the Loire valley, a relatively rare beast in that part of France. The advice was to have it chilled, so we did. It was exquisite.

Minutes later, we were whisked to our table and orders were taken.

It was turning into an evening of indecision. My wife was torn between the fish and shellfish soup, with Gruyère cheese and croutons, and the grilled mussels with three cheeses. Eric said either would satisfy, but when pushed, advised the mussels.

I needed no assistance as I opted for the breast of wood pigeon, served on a bed of beetroot with a forest fruit and port sauce. While it sounded like gout on a plate, the blend of flavours and textures worked perfectly.

Just like Eric's advice. The mussels, served out of the shell in a dish which resembled a circular ice cube tray, each had their own delicious helping of the pungent cheese. They were to die for.

On to the main courses. My wife, with assistance again, chose the monkfish bourgignon, while my own preference was the lamb shank with mash and a red wine sauce. We ordered a side portion of vegetables and French fries – not chips.

The lamb fell off the bone in its pursuit of the creamy mash and rich, flavoursome sauce. The French fries helped mop up the vast quantity of sauce surrounding the monkfish, which wasn't terribly abundant but did become the latest holder of the "that's the best monkfish I have ever tasted" title.

Was there room for dessert? If **Café Tabou** could squeeze in an impossible number of diners, we could manage a sweet end to the evening. Eric made it a stress-free night for my wife by choosing one of the evening's specials, a trio of chocolate torte. Determined to immerse myself fully in the Gallic flavour of the evening, I decided to test out the crêpe suzette.

As the flames died on my plate, I delved into this bittersweet mixture of orange, pancake and alcohol, cooled by proper vanilla ice cream.

The torte was declared smoother than Sean Connery in his best James Bond dinner jacket, and a degree tastier as well.

So caught up in the buzzing entente cordiale atmosphere were we, two coffees were ordered to round off the evening, but we couldn't decide between Cognac and Armagnac. By this stage, Eric didn't ask. He just arrived with two glasses which could have doubled as a home for stray goldfish, and a few minutes later, almost as an afterthought, produced a bottle to let us know what we had been drinking. Grand Armagnac.

It was fantastic value for the quality not just of the food, wine and service, but also for the feeling that we had experienced an excellent night out. Try it, and don't forget to ask for Eric.

Quality of Food	5
Menu Choice	4
Surroundings	4
Location	4
Service	5
Value for Money	5
Total *[out of 30]*	**27**

Hamish's

Glenfiddich House, Main Street, Methven

telephone: 01738 840505   website: www.hamishs.co.uk

"Two hours of heaven"

The village of Methven, straddling the road between Perth and Crieff, has had a long and colourful past.

Whether that is the reason for **Hamish's** restaurant to have such a vivid, one might say bloody, red interior, I know not.

The choice of wall and seat colouring had provoked considerable conversation between the two of us. My guest liked it and found it rather trendy and, dare I say, minimalist when taken in with surroundings.

I wasn't quite so sure, and must admit I still have my doubts, especially now I know that

Robert The Bruce was defeated by the Earl of Pembroke at Methven in 1306 and that, in 1644, 2,500 warriors died at the Battle of Tibbermore.

Whatever the inspiration for the colour, it was the signal for something very different, which to me, personifies **Hamish's**.

This is not your normal country restaurant in a big, old house with creaking floorboards and stuffy, aged staff.

Instead, **Hamish's**, like the interior decor, is somewhat in your face. One could say bright, brash and very different in that you would expect to find this type of eatery in a swanky city centre, not a tiny village six miles west of Perth.

If it were located in Edinburgh, it would have been filled to capacity on the midweek night on which we dined rather than just the two of us and a group of teachers, judging by their conversation, some tables distant.

I'd passed by **Hamish's** on many occasions, but this particular evening its bright blue outside lights proved too big a magnet.

The menu was simple, but very impressive. The chef obviously has a passion because not every restaurant in the world would be able to get away with macaroni and cheese as a starter.

To me, that proved the biggest draw. To adulterate the words of one well-known TV advertisement, this was not just any macaroni and cheese, this was **Hamish's** macaroni cheese with a herb and Parmesan crust and pieces of wonderfully crisp Parma ham, too.

It came beautifully presented and was devoured with considerable pleasure. It could be said I was in heaven.

My dining companion spent some time considering whether it would be the tartlet of crab, the roast pigeon and pheasant boudin or the steamed west coast mussels and smoked bacon with garlic, shallot and white-wine cream sauce.

He opted for the mussels in the end and was not disappointed. In fact, I was jealous. My macaroni had stimulated the taste buds, but his mussels drove them into overdrive as the sauce, which had just a hint of dill, proved magnificent.

Indeed, dill proved to be the herb of the day, or so it seemed, because it appeared with my main course, too.

I'd debated for some time about the main and whether I would go for the meat or fish. In the end, the monkfish won over the corn-fed chicken accompanied with a garlic herb mousse, and the braised lamb shank that sounded divine with its grainy mustard and roasted root vegetable and served with stock juices.

My monkfish was cooked to absolute perfection, retaining a delightful bite. The accompaniments, a confit of fennel, boulangère potatoes and a dill hollandaise, were delicious.

My guest also had a long debate over his main, but in the end went for roast breast of mallard served on celeriac potato rôsti with a red onion jam and game reduction. The mallard was served medium and he enjoyed it, too.

We shouldn't have had desserts, but did. I had the cheese and biscuit selection with a large pot of tea while my companion went for a Border tart, a very fruity creation served with what proved to be a real eye-opener and taste sensation, ginger and honey ice cream.

I was driving, so wine was declined. Selfish it may have been, but I took the stance that if I couldn't enjoy a drink then neither could my guest.

Instead, we had a bottle of sparkling water which, disappointingly, came not from the fridge, but from a cupboard two tables away. It was warm.

That was my only complaint about **Hamish's** in what otherwise proved to be a two-hour food sensation.

Quality of Food	5
Menu Choice	5
Surroundings	5
Location	4
Service	4
Value for Money	5
Total [out of 30]	**28**

Yann's at Glenearn House

Perth Road, Crieff

telephone: 01764 650111   website: www.yannsatglenearn house.com

"Yann's on the ball"

It had been one of those awful days when the Scottish rugby team gave the game away.

Had the four penalty kicks

against South Africa been converted then your restaurant reviewer – and a legion of other Scottish fans – might have left Murrayfield just a tad happier.

Thankfully, the team at **Yann's** at Glenearn House, Crieff, were on the ball later as we headed home. Their performance in providing the necessary comfort food was in stark contrast to Scotland's woeful kickers.

Yann's, a restaurant with rooms, has a very distinctive French feel thanks to owners Yannick and Shari Grospellier. Yann was born in Haute Savoi, in the French Alps, and started cooking aged thirteen, making crêpes at his parents' restaurant in Chamonix.

The couple had made a considerable effort earlier in the day to accommodate us. Yes, I left the booking late and called them just before I left for Edinburgh.

The response was unsurprising in that they thought they had a full house. They would, however, check and call back. Ten minutes later, we were booked in, provided we ate at 6.30pm and left by 8pm.

We initially passed by the eatery on Crieff's Perth Road; its sign is not that distinctive. However, we found it on our second pass and were quickly ushered into the very comfortable lounge and its hearty open fire by a waiter who had just arrived for work. The TV had on the Ireland against the All Blacks match. We were in heaven – and that wasn't the result of the rather generous pre-dinner glasses of wine.

The menu had a distinctive Gallic twist. French onion soup, crêpe Provençale and la tartiflette (traditional alpine gratin of potatoes, pancetta and reblochon cheese) were there to tempt the taste buds. More ambitious was la fondue Savoyarde for two, although I doubted if the pan of melted comté cheese and crusty bread would have done much to resolve my hunger pangs.

That said, had I been on the ball we could have pre-ordered la pierrade, which consisted of a hot Italian slate, a "big platter of meat" (chicken, beef, lamb, pork and duck), a bowl of salad, chips and a selection of sauces that included aioli and Dijonnaise.

After two hours in Murrayfield's west stand, there was only one starter for the two of us – French onion soup. My rugby friend chose the chicken pie, which was that night's special, for his main, while I opted for the roast monkfish, pilaff rice and chive sauce.

The soup proved amazing and was a meal in itself, with a generous helping of melted cheese, bread and onions. It went down a treat and was just what was required to inject some heat into a cold body.

The monkfish – wrapped in bacon – was just a little overcooked for my liking, but nevertheless tasted fine. The accompanying side salad was boosted by a wonderful and oh-so-delicious French dressing.

He who ordered the traditional French chicken pie had by far the best main. It came served boiling hot in a very large bowl. The pastry top hid what I was told was a delightful combination of chicken, vegetables, mushrooms and ham. He obviously enjoyed it as it was demolished with vigour.

We passed on the desserts, instead selecting the biscuits and cheese and sharing a pot of tea. The cheese was a selection of both Scottish and French. Amazingly, there were more than enough biscuits.

Glenearn House is a former dorm for Crieff's private Morrison's Academy. That explains the huge clock on the dining-room wall.

The restaurant was very busy, confirmation that it is exceptionally popular. We were impressed with the decoration and the meal, albeit that, at one point, a not-on-the-ball waitress decided to pour tap water into our glasses of sparkling water.

More impressive, though, was being able to watch Yann and his assistant at work in the kitchen. There was no drama. Both were focused on delivering quality food and in ensuring that it was sent out to the tables quickly. Healthy rapeseed oil was the oil of choice in the cooking.

Our meal was tremendous value for money.

Quality of Food	4
Menu Choice	4
Surroundings	5
Location	4
Service	4
Value for Money	5
Total [out of 30]	**26**

More reviews every Saturday in the *Press and Journal*